This circa 1855 view of
Wilmington appeared in Gleason's
Pictorial Drawing Room
Companion. It depicts a thriving
port city. Courtesy, John Robert
Lane, Jr.

Cape Fear Adventure

An Illustrated History of Wilmington

◆ ◆ ◆

By Diane Cobb Cashman

◆ ◆ ◆

Pictorial Research by Lynn W. Graham
With Color Photography by Freda Hartness Wilkins
"Partners in Progress" by James Robert Warren
Produced in Cooperation with the
Lower Cape Fear Historical Society, Inc.

◆ ◆ ◆

Windsor Publications
Woodland Hills, California

Windsor Publications
History Books Division

Publisher: John M. Phillips
Editorial Director: Lissa Sanders
Administrative Coordinator: Katherine Cooper
Senior Picture Editor: Teri Davis Greenberg
Senior Corporate History Editor: Karen Story
Production Manager: James Burke
Art Director: Alexander D'Anca
Art Production Manager: Dee Cooper
Composition Manager: E. Beryl Myers

Staff for *Cape Fear Adventure*
Editor: Pamela Taylor
Designer: Phil Waters
Assistant Editor: Todd Ackerman
Picture Editor: Teri Davis Greenberg
Editorial Assistants: Susan Block, Patricia Dailey,
   Phyllis Gray, Henriette Henderson, Karen Holroyd,
   Mary Mohr, Susan Wells
Production Artists: Beth Bowman, Ellen Hazeltine, Chris McKibbin
Typographers: Shannon Mellies, Barbara Neiman

The vessels George Davis,
Roseville, *and* Pensher *load up at
Sprunt's Champion Compress and
Warehouse Company wharves in
Wilmington. This engraving
appeared in the Cape Fear and
Yadkin Valley edition of the*
Wilmington Messenger.
*Courtesy, North Carolina State
Archives*

Contents

In 1663 Captain William Hilton scouted the Cape Fear River and reported
". . . as good as land well timbered as any we have seen in any other part of
the world, sufficient to accommodate thousands of our English nation . . ."
A few months later settlers arrived and established the trading post Charles
Town (center) on the west bank of the river at Old Town Creek. Courtesy,
North Carolina State Archives

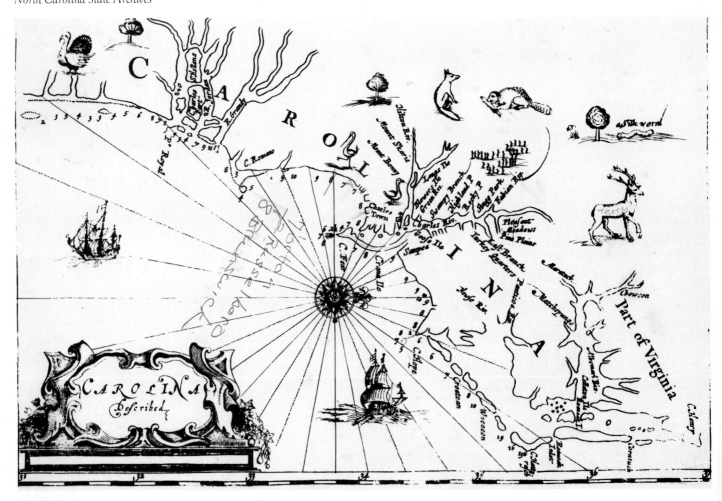

Introduction

> What his imagination is to the poet, facts are to the historian.
> His exercise of judgement comes in their selection, his art is in their
> arrangement, his method is narrative. His subject is the story of man's
> past. His function is to make it known.
>
> —Barbara W. Tuchman, *Practicing History*

For over a quarter century the Lower Cape Fear Historical Society, Inc. has "made known" the history of this region through its archives, Latimer House Museum, programs, publications, seminars, and tours. With the publication of *Cape Fear Adventure* it hopes to reach a new, larger audience who will have an opportunity to learn more about the history and heritage of the place where they live or vacation.

It was a personal honor to be entrusted with the responsibility of writing the narrative, but I was audacious enough to try because so many outstanding historical studies were available and so many experts were willing to share the burden of research with me. The facts which document this area's past are found in diaries, letters, journals, military dispatches, statistical surveys, newspapers, photographs, paintings, museums, individuals' recollections, dissertations, published monographs, and texts, as well as the articles which have appeared in the Society's *Bulletin.* Ferreting out these facts became an agreeable pursuit which brought me in contact with accommodating archivists, curators, historians, librarians, and individual citizens who shared their ideas, collections, memories, and expertise. My search also took me to every place described and I gained a wide range of stimulating experiences, from looking at the Judah Benjamin file in the cool vaults of the Historic New Orleans Collection, or rocking and listening in the book-lined room of Miss Elizabeth McKoy, to cleaning off gravestones in the quiet churchyard of St. James, Goose Creek, South Carolina. Early on in this project I made a formal request for help in locating unpublished materials and photographs. People proved generous and much of the anecdotal inclusions and some of the pictures are a result of that yield.

As my research progressed and my notes outgrew their file drawers it became increasingly difficult to determine what to retain for the text. For example, I was charmed by Thomas Fanning Wood's botanical notes, which charted the timetable of daffodil blooms, and Joseph Swift's observation that Anna MacNeill Whistler's mother, Martha Kingsley, was "the most beautiful and interesting woman in Wilmington"—but both finds were excised because I was trying to trim rather than fatten. Sometimes when I least expected it a tidbit would surface to corroborate a historical event. My favorite was found in Harmon Rorison's scrapbook, which stated that on a

World War II Friday payday, an emergency exit had to be cut through the wall of the Security National Bank so that the depositors could get out. What could more graphically describe the bulge of those prosperous war years?

As the manuscript took shape I had moments of doubt and discouragement because I lost confidence in my "exercise of judgement" and "art of arrangement." Fortunately, the Society's readers, the Windsor editors, and my family and friends always knew when to spur me or cheer me. To those special cheerleaders I send my thanks.

I am particularly grateful to those who read the manuscript in its entirety—Betty H. Boney, James O. and Rosalie Carr, Margaret T. Hall, Melton McLaurin, and Leora (Billie) McEachern, and to those who critiqued the chapters or segments related to their specialty—Christopher Fonvielle, Thomas Loftfield, E.M. McEachern, Beverley Tetterton, and Alan D. Watson. I also made many a query and R.V. Asbury, Ed Danilowicz, Andrew H. Harriss, Jr., Henry Jay MacMillan, William S. Powell, Dorothy Ray, Bill Reaves, and Janet Seapker graciously responded with quick answers. Charles H. Boney helped photographer Freda Wilkins with some of the architectural shots. Bill Reaves edited the captions and Jerry Blow brought some very old gray photos back into focus. Much of the last chapter is based on personal interviews cited in the bibliography and on Robert M. Fales' slide lectures and videotapes of "what he saw and heard" in days gone by.

Cape Fear Adventure has been a cooperative project of the Society which was first suggested by president Isabel M. Williams. It has been in the works through the presidencies of Landon B. Anderson, Betty H. Boney, and Capt. Frank S. Conlon, and each has enthusiastically coordinated the efforts of the Society with Windsor Publications. The actual book is the combined work of Freda Wilkins, Lynn Graham, James Robert Warren, and myself, and we have pooled our information and ideas and relied upon our editors, Lissa Sanders, Pam Taylor, Teri Greenberg, and Karen Story, who supervised the final "art of arrangement." None of this would have been possible without our sponsors, whose stories are told in "Partners in Progress."

On the personal side, I have enjoyed the loyal, loving support of John, Nancy, and Patrick Cashman, who recognized that this project afforded me a great personal adventure and who provided the means to let me have it.

Diane C. Cashman
Wilmington, North Carolina
June 1982

The Land is Found and Forfeited:

North Carolina's mightiest river, the Cape Fear, widens and churns with swelling tides in its last few miles before entering the sea at the place where the state's southernmost cape juts out into the Atlantic—at 33 degrees 50′ northern latitude. Over the centuries mounds of coquinas, shifting sandbars, and silt have built up at this junction of river and sea, forming a series of shoals (long known as the Frying Pan Shoals) extending out from shore some 20 miles. In order to enter the river one must first secure safe passage over the shoals and then thread one's way across the shifting sandbars at the river's mouth. Navigation here has always been hazardous, with many a shipwreck to document the treachery of the southern extreme of the "Graveyard of the Atlantic." To this day only a knowledgeable pilot can ease large ships into the river and up the stream the 28 miles to Wilmington.

The landfall has been known by many names, and has been the subject of controversy for centuries. An ancient map uses the Latin *Promontorium Tremendum* to denote the cape, which has also been charted Feare, San Romano, and Fair. From the cape's name came the river's name, or at least the name we use today, for the river also has been given many names. To the Indians who lived on its western branch above the fall line, it was the Sapona; to the Spanish, the Rio Jordan; to the New Englanders and Barbadians, the Charles and Cape Fear; to later settlers, the Clarendon; and to the optimists, the Cape Fair. A poet called it "the Golden River" and it has surely been the Port City of Wilmington's greatest treasure.

The Cape Fear's navigable stream was the natural highway that led from the Atlantic upstream to where the river divided into two branches, the northwest stream being called the Cape Fear River and northeast stream the Northeast River. Just below the forks, across from Eagles' Island on the river's eastern bank, the town of Wilmington would emerge, as the river's potential attracted settlers. Its waters provided the means for transportation, commerce, and communication, and nurtured the people and animals who lived near its shores—an area so distinctive as to seem to be its own little realm.

The visitor to modern Wilmington might only see a charming city on low sandy hills above the Cape Fear River; the more astute and the "old" Wilmingtonian recognizes that here is a place where centuries of history have left their mark—modern buildings exist harmoniously with ballast walls, 19th-century mansions, and iron-front fences. Shady brick streets and tree-lined plazas turn into busy thoroughfares, and near the sea, sound roads loop past developments such as Pirate's Cove where buccaneers purportedly hid treasure.

The land and seascape of the Lower Cape Fear still provide scenes of splendored beauty—egrets glide over the salt marshes while herons stand one-legged in the sedge; kingfishers dive for their dinner; sea turtles make tracks in the sand as they follow the light of the full moon to lay their eggs above the high tide mark; and cypresses, garlanded with moss, admire their stately reflections in dark swamp mirrors. But the land that greeted the first humans thousands of years ago was even more lush in its variety. Carolina parakeets flitted through deep woods, turkeys' gobbles echoed through the primeval forest, huge sturgeon swam upstream to spawn in the river, and pine wilderness stretched toward every horizon.

The first human beings to hunt and gather here fashioned their shelters from vines and tree boughs. It is believed that the hunting was very good for these people, who left behind spears (thrown from weighted *atlatls*), stone projectile points, stone tools, and animal bones. Their descendants used bows and arrows and fired-clay pottery, the remnants of which archaeologists now use to trace their movements. These Indians were skilled fishermen, devising traps, intricate nets, and other devices to harvest the rich bounty from the waters of the ocean and river. The shell mounds they left behind document their feasts. They also discovered the purgative power of the Yaupon leaf tea and annually "renewed" themselves by brewing the "Black Drink."

Mystery shrouds the origins and ancestors of these Indians; we do not even know what name they gave to themselves. It is believed that they can be linked linguistically with the Siouan-speaking Indians—the Waccamaws share this heritage—it is even possible that a few Indians with Algonquian background might have lived in the region. Yet, although these early Cape Fear residents did not leave their name upon the land or the water, they did leave a lasting imprint on the land.

The Indians used fire to increase the land's yield. Great fires burned out the undergrowth, forcing animals out of their brier-patch coverings and laying bare the earth for planting. As the Indians burned over the land year after year, the forest was renewed and grasses thrived as pocosins and broad savannahs took shape.

The first European eyewitness description of the Cape Fear and its native inhabitants was written by a Florentine in the service of the French flag; his arrival marked an important turning point in area history, even though the fruits of his visit were long in coming.

The date is March 1, 1524. Giovanni da Verrazano, two months earlier, had been given a convoy of four ships by Francis I, who believed the 38-year-old gentleman navigator when he promised to find a route to Asia that would be faster than the present one, through the Straits of Magellan. It has been a fearful voyage: three ships are gone, and his own—*La Dauphine*—has just come through a fierce storm. The tempest has blown him to the point which he has noted in his log: "Landfall, 34 degrees N." The "happy shores of Cathay" it was not; it was the mouth of the Cape Fear River.

Verrazano soon started upstream. The land-burnings of the Indians attracted his attention and he ordered a shore party to disembark at the spot local tradition places at Orton Plantation. The captain recorded his observations in a long letter prepared for the French king. He praised the beauty of the land, declaring it a place "as pleasant and delectable to behold as it is possible to imagine." He described the sensuous fragrance of bay laurel in the air, which caused

him to name the place *Selva di Lauri* (forest of laurels); and noted the "russet" inhabitants of the spot who, he said, were peaceful and hospitable:

> They are well featured in their limbs, of mean stature, and somewhat bigger than we; broadbreasted, strong armed, their legs and other parts of their body well fashioned, and they are disfigured in nothing.

After enough of the land and its people had been observed to make a report to his sponsors, Verrazano turned *La Dauphine* north to scout the upper reaches of the Eastern Seaboard, including the future site of New York City.

The Spanish, extremely busy exploring and conquering parts of the New World in the 16th century, made a brief attempt to colonize coastal North Carolina under the leadership of Lucas Vasquez de Ayllón, but rusty remnants of armor were all they left behind in the land called Chicora, then Allyón (after their leader, who succumbed to fever here).

The next—and last—colonial power to claim and colonize the Carolinas was England, whose bold and mighty Queen Elizabeth decreed her right to all lands not inhabited by Christian princes or peoples. She gave Walter Raleigh permission to plant a colony (alas, another failure) in "Virginia." But it was not until the 17th century that this land became of any real importance to the Crown.

In 1629 Charles I granted a vast tract of American real estate to his attorney general, Sir Robert Heath, who, to honor his sovereign, rechristened the Land of Allyón to Carolana (Charles' land). Heath eventually transferred the patent, and Charles was executed after a bloody civil war in 1649; but the land was not forgotten and came to the attention of a group of New England Puritans who sought to colonize in a territory more temperate than Massachusetts.

A group of these Massachusetts Bay colonists formed the Adventurers about Cape Fayre, and employed Captain William Hilton, a mariner of distinguished reputation, to explore the southern seaboard that had been described in London broadsides of the previous century as "The Goodliest Soil Under the Cope of Heaven." It was in the first week of October 1662 that Hilton eased his ship, the *Adventure,* up the river to the site where Wilmington was later to be founded.

Hilton was immediately enthusiastic, proclaiming the place "the most temperate of the temperate zones." While Hilton took notes, a crew member made the findings, and when they returned to Massachusetts, the first detailed map of the Lower Cape Fear was executed by Nicholas Shapley, although it is not known if Shapley accompanied the expedition.

Hilton convinced his sponsors that they should settle the area without delay; but this colony, like so many others in the dangerous and isolated New World, was short-lived. For reasons that still are not completely clear they soon abandoned the place. (It may have been due, in part, to the news that Puritan rule in England had come to an end, and the Puritans feared reprisals from the new King Charles II.)

Undaunted by this turn of events, Captain Hilton turned his talents of persuasion upon a new group of speculators—not Puritans this time—in overcrowded Barbados. In 1663 he convinced these

Above: *Catesby and Bartram admired the stately heron, a bird that enchanted visitors to the Lower Cape Fear area in the 17th and 18th centuries as much as it does today. From* Catesby's Natural History of Carolina, Florida, and the Bahama Islands. *Courtesy, Beehive Press, Savannah, Georgia*
Above right: *The Venus Flytrap, shown in this William Bartram sketch, is very rare and is found only in the coastal areas of the Carolinas. Courtesy, American*

Philosophical Society
Top: *Naturalist Bartram sketched this alligator, perhaps while it was basking in the sun on the bank of his uncle William's plantation on the Cape Fear River. Courtesy, American Philosophical Society*
Right: *Early explorer John Lawson illustrated his* A New Voyage to Carolina *with sketches of beasts likely to be encountered in the Carolinas. Courtesy, North Carolina State Archives*

wealthy planters to take a gamble on the Cape Fear. Charles II was in the process of conveying the old Heath land grant to eight of his supporters—the Lords Proprietors, who would govern the Carolinas until 1729. On August 12, 1663, the newly formed Barbadian Corporation sent a petition, signed by 200 people, requesting the Lords Proprietors to grant them permission to settle at Cape Fear.

Hilton, along with Captain Anthony Long and Peter Fabian, returned to the Cape Fear to further explore the area. It was at this time that Hilton gave names that still endure to two places: Rocky Point and Sugar Loaf. As Verrazano before him had done, Hilton met with the Indians of the area; and he formally purchased the land and river from the chief, Wattcoosa.

Hilton returned to Barbados with an even more glowing account of the place than he had submitted before. One who was soundly convinced to colonize was John Vassal, who decided to lead the first group of Barbadian planters, with their slaves, to the Cape Fear. Arriving on May 24, 1664, they soon incorporated the region as County Clarendon (named after one of the Lords Proprietors). Such flattering gestures did not greatly ease the complexities of achieving a good working agreement with the Proprietors, however; although their leader, Vassal, was appointed deputy governor, their political troubles were far from nonexistent.

The colonists were fully occupied with the rigors of clearing land, building houses, and coping with the many adjustments, such as a large mosquito population. Eventually the newcomers made progress, building a trading post called Charles Town, carrying on a brisk trade in barrel staves with the West Indies, and harvesting several good crops. Word reached London of their bounty, resulting in an account, printed in London in 1664, of "... a New Plantation begun by the English at Cape Feare ..."

> They have a naturally growing abundance of the most stately timber of most sorts in England, but very many other sorts not known to us, as cedar, sassafras, and other sweet woods; vines, also mulberry and olive trees, from whence come the three rich commodities of wine, silk, and oil. They have abundance of turkeys and other fowls in the woods, and great stores of sturgeon, salmon, and many other sorts of other good eating fish, both flat and round.

By the time word started to spread of the colonists' good fortune, however, the demise of the colony was already beginning. It happened that Vassal had been too hasty in his colonization of the Cape Fear: the Lords Proprietors, it seems, were not yet thoroughly convinced that they should considerably support this particular Carolina colony. Vassal's arch-rival, John Yeamans, ingratiated himself with the faction of Proprietors who favored settlement in the Port Royal area of what is now South Carolina. When Yeamans was knighted by Charles II and made governor of County Clarendon, Vassal lost even more effectiveness in getting much-needed aid for his colony: Yeamans made it clear that he himself favored supporting the Port Royal settlement.

Politics of another sort became a problem for the colonists of County Clarendon, too. County residents' attempt to make slaves of some Cape Fear Indians soon resulted in retaliation against the whole colony. Cattle disappeared, seedlings were turned over, fields were trampled, and stray arrows found their marks. Virtually abandoned by England and threatened by their Indian neighbors, the struggling band along 60 miles of river banks were starting to desert the homes they had so recently built. Vassal, in London, tried to get assistance for them, but most Londoners—preoccupied with the effects of the Great Plague, and then the Fire, of 1666—were little interested in the problems of colonists 3,000 miles away.

By the summer of 1667 it was apparent, even to Vassal, that County Clarendon was doomed. Many of its residents, however, relocated to the area which had won out as the recipient of Proprietary help. Some of their descendants now live in Charleston, South Carolina.

The last colonists to leave by ship watched the headland of the Cape Fear drop away from view by the end of 1667. The homes they abandoned were soon overgrown by Southern smilax and Carolina jessamine. Brick chimneys toppled and crumbled on the ground below while pinestraw and acorns carpeted the soil that had once been cultivated. Civilization's hallmarks—pewter spoons, buttons, Delftware, pipe stems, coins, and nails—were buried in the accumulating layers of mulch; reclaimed, as was the land itself, by the wilderness.

◆ ◆ ◆

John White sketched the Indian practice of placing earth mounds in canoes topped by fire to provide light to gig flounder. The Indians also built weirs, stake-like dams, in stream channels to trap fish. From De Bry, Thomas Hariot's Virginia

This illustration from an ancient Spanish history book depicts the 1525 Cape Fear landing of Lucas Vasquez de Ayllon. It is believed that Ayllon's expedition produced two "firsts" in the New World—the building of a new ship at Cape Fear and a Christian religious service, which was held after one of the ships foundered on the shoals. Courtesy, North Carolina State Archives

With the restoration of the monarchy in 1663, Charles II was placed on the English throne. The king rewarded his political supporters with the old Heath grant of American real estate, which he renamed for himself— Carolana. Courtesy, North Carolina State Archives

Chapter II
Pirates and Planters:

As the 17th century drew to a close, the men "of color russet" no longer found the white man fascinating or attractive but rather an abominable enemy to be eradicated. The Cape Fear Indians proved to have long memories, and time, instead of erasing the scars of their betrayal by the Clarendon settlers, only festered the wounds, driving them to brutal massacres of the white man wherever he was found. Although the region of the Cape Fear lay deserted until the early decades of the 18th century, grisly tales of the Indians' attacks upon shipwrecked sailors or traders who wandered into the region further tarnished the darkening reputation of the Cape Fear.

There were other men, however, who were fairly oblivious to the white-red relations of the region for their interests lay not upon the land, but upon the waters off the Cape Fear. The mouth of the Cape Fear River had become a gathering place for pirates in what has been termed "the golden age of piracy" in the early 18th century. These marauders sailed in brigantines, shallops, and sloops bearing such names as *Revenge, Fancy,* and *Adventure.* Their exploits have been romanticized into a regional legacy of legend and folklore.

Cape Fear offered the pirates a primitive drydock and shipyard, and an ideal place for careening, whereby a ship would be driven aground, pushed over, cleaned of barnacles and repaired. The shoreline's coves, inlets, and islands also provided a safe haven for the pirates before sailing out to capture an unsuspecting ship along the coast. North Carolina's most famous pirate was Edward Drummond of Bristol, England (also known by the alias Teach, or Thatch), who came to be known—and deeply feared—as Blackbeard.

Blackbeard's home base of operation was Pamlico and Albemarle sounds, but he sailed the waters off the coast of Cape Fear and eventually became a comrade-in-arms with the Cape Fear's most famous pirate, Stede Bonnet. While Major Stede Bonnet of Barbados had been a conventional gentleman, he became an unconventional pirate. Known as "the Gentleman Pirate," it was reputedly his nagging wife who drove him from the drawing room to the brigantine. He brought to the occupation little more than enthusiasm for a life of adventure, and a ship, the *Revenge,* which he had purchased, not captured. Although Bonnet was vastly ignorant of piratical skills, he managed to capture some ships loaded with booty and to catch the eye of Blackbeard, who invited him to become an ally. For a brief time Bonnet and Blackbeard plundered together, but the Barbadian's inexperience and gullibility were so obvious that Blackbeard couldn't resist taking over operations. Eventually, Bonnet was able to part company with Blackbeard and headed south to the mouth of the Cape Fear, a decision which was later to prove a miscalculation.

While the region of the Cape Fear remained a lonely wilderness into the early part of the 18th century, settlements in the Carolinas developed into towns. Beaufort, New Bern, Bath, and Edenton to the north prospered and to the south, the busy port of Charleston flourished. In 1718 Blackbeard, with a contingent of more than 400 pirates, including Bonnet, led a daring blockade of Charleston. Pirates even walked the streets of the city, terrorizing the inhabitants. When citizens of South Carolina and Virginia—angry and humiliated that their coastal towns had become the easy target of marauders—pressured governors Alexander Spotswood of Virginia and Robert Johnson of South Carolina to rid the coast of these criminals, both governors decided to launch expeditions to eradicate Blackbeard and Bonnet.

A pirate named Robert Vane had been harassing Charleston and rumor had it that he was hiding out at Cape Fear. When Colonel William Rhett of Charleston volunteered to seek out Vane and destroy him, a grateful Governor Johnson gladly authorized an expedition to Cape Fear. Rhett's party reached the mouth of the Cape Fear on September 26, 1718. A ship's mast was spied and Rhett cautiously approached in anticipation of surprising Vane. But upon confrontation, Rhett discovered that he had come upon an even bigger catch, Major Stede Bonnet. The Charlestonians and the pirates engaged in a fierce struggle, the shifting Cape Fear sandbars serving as battleground. Ships would go aground, only to break free again as the sandbars see-sawed between the tides. Finally Rhett subdued Bonnet at the place now known as Bonnet's Creek in modern day Southport, North Carolina. Some of the pirates scrambled into the forest, and legend has it that a few of these survivors were absorbed into an Indian tribe to the northwest, for in later years some English-speaking Indians were encountered in that area. While other pirates lay dead and dying upon the deck, the living were bound, along with their chagrined captain, and their captor, William Rhett, returned triumphantly to Charleston.

Since he was a gentleman, Bonnet was not incarcerated with his crew. He took advantage of this class distinction, which allowed him separate quarters, and he was able to arrange a successful escape to nearby Sullivan's Island. Bonnet's freedom was short-lived, however, and he was recaptured and returned to a more secure holding place in Charleston. Bonnet knew that he had played out his last card and the former buccaneer disintegrated into a pathetic, broken man who cried and pleaded for mercy. His distress aroused pity and some efforts were made to pressure the governor to rescind the death penalty; however, Johnson was firm in his resolve to prove that piracy did not pay. On December 10, 1718, a weeping Bonnet emerged from his prison; a sympathizer pushed a nosegay into his manacled hands as he was led to the gallows. He was given the traditional pirate's funeral and was buried below the low tidewater mark at Charleston's waterfront. Today, tourists walk the battery above the site of the Gentleman Pirate's watery grave.

Meanwhile, Virginia's governor, Alexander Spotswood, had appointed Captain Ellis Brand to lead an expedition—with Lieutenant Robert Maynard in command of two sloops—to seek out and destroy the infamous Blackbeard. Maynard and Blackbeard met off Ocracoke Island. Blackbeard's *Adventure* did not have its full complement of crew (the crew had dwindled because Blackbeard was not, at

Edward Drummond was a name that struck terror into the heart of every sailor of the early 18th century. Also known by the alias Teach or Thatch, Drummond was more colorfully known as Blackbeard. When preparing for battle, it is reported he tucked slow-burning tapers behind his ears to speed the firing of his cannon. He may also have done this to exaggerate his already menacing appearance. Courtesy, North Carolina State Archives

the time, actively engaged in plundering on the high seas). Between 18 and 25 members remained; one third of the pirates were black and each was armed with a cutlass and pistols. Maynard's sloops were well-armed and primed for the fight. Blackbeard had spent the night drinking and when he spied the alien ships he barked, "Damn you for villains, who are you? And from whence come you?" The reply from Maynard caused Blackbeard to order *Adventure's* eight cannons to fire such powerful broadside that his own ship was thrust back upon the shore. Maynard realized that another broadside would do them in, so he ordered a defensive maneuver which would force Blackbeard to come to him. The crew was sent below deck to await the arrival of the pirates. Blackbeard arrived, along with a store of his version of the grenade—one of his own inventions, consisting of a bottle filled with shot and powder, ignited by a fuse. The primitive grenades were thrown on the enemy's deck to incite chaos. But the ploy did not work since Maynard's men were below. A frustrated Blackbeard then ordered out the grappling irons and the *Adventure* was lashed to the sloop. With Blackbeard in the lead, a party of 11 boarded the ship. When Maynard gave the signal, his crewmen poured from the hold and a bloody battle ensued. The deck was awash with blood and a witness reported that even the seawater around the ship took on a red stain. Blackbeard fought like a demon and engaged Maynard in a man-to-man fight to the death. The pirate's ferocious endurance allowed him to sustain five pistol wounds and 20 severe cuts before he fell to the deck and died. About half the *Adventure's* crew (nine had been killed) abandoned ship and begged for mercy but their days were numbered. They were later tried and hanged outside Williamsburg. Maynard hung Blackbeard's head from his ship's bowsprit as a warning to those who might be foolish enough to engage in pirating.

In the years that followed, there were still some who thought a pirate's life might be the way to easy riches, but the deaths of Bonnet and Blackbeard acted as a real deterrent to would-be pirates. The government's crackdown on their hiding places and operations ended the widespread piracy of the period, although local legends of pirates still abound. Money Island—which lies one mile southwest of Wrightsville Beach off Greenville Sound—got its name because of the persistent stories of pirates' hidden treasure. Generations of treasure-seekers have spaded the sand in hopes of finding the buried chests of gold. And tales have always been told of taking Spanish gold from some pirate cache at Sloop Point, near Topsail. There have even been stories of wives of Blackbeard operating a tavern and suspected bordello out of present-day Southport. Over the years the Lower Cape Fear's poets, playwrights, storytellers, and journalists have told of the pirates who once made the region a port of call. The historians place the end of "the golden age of piracy" at around 1720, but the legacy of pirate legend has grown in local imagination with every passing year. The grim realities of life in the Cape Fear wilderness needed no embellishment. Notations from old maps, property deeds and transfers, place names, and stories provide clues to the fates of people and places that were a part of the Lower Cape Fear's earliest history. After the debacle of County Clarendon, it was considered folly to try to make a go of it in the wilderness, although records of early attempts at settlement do exist, along with a number of legends. One legend explains the origin of Lockwood's Folly in Brunswick County by saying that a man named Lockwood tried to settle there and trade with

the Indians, only to be killed. The 1662 Nicholas Shapley map from the Hilton expedition poses another puzzle, for it shows an outline of James Fort on the east bank of the Cape Fear River, near the site of present-day Wilmington, but one can only speculate as to whether a fort ever existed.

Around 1714 adjoining land tracts on the Northeast Cape Fear River, about 80 miles above the forks, were granted to Welshmen John Hughes, Price Hughes, Thomas James, and Enoch Morgan. This settlement has always been designated the Welsh Tract and more of this group came in the 1730s. But the settlement was burnt and the early Welsh settlers murdered by Indians.

The Lower Cape Fear had little appeal to colonizers while life in the wilderness was so tenuous, although attempts had been made by the government in South Carolina to negotiate a truce with the Indians of the Cape Fear. For a while the Cape Fear Indians did cooperate, even providing manpower during the Tuscarora War—aiding expeditions from the Carolinas and Virginia in suppressing the hostile Iroquoian-speaking Indians who had settled near Raleigh. But the Yamassee War of 1715 found the Cape Fear Indians back on the warpath, as they joined the Yamassee and other Indians in fighting the English. James Moore and his brother, Maurice Moore, of South Carolina both provided the leadership that finally suppressed the Indians. When Maurice Moore discovered the murdered settlers of the Welsh Tract, he extracted a confession from one of the Indians. As a result, Moore organized a force to seek out, capture, and destroy the Cape Fear Indians. His foray was a success, and he brought his captives back to Charleston. Maurice Moore not only was to prove himself a fierce Indian fighter, whose personality and conquests made his name a legend to both red and white inhabitants of the Carolinas but he was also a skillful diplomat who could sit down and convince the Indians to act in the settlers' interests. Moore persuaded the Cherokees, for example, to support the South Carolina colonists rather than join with the Creeks in war against them. This action effectively ended the Yamassee War and by 1724 it was reported that most of the Cape Fear Indians had moved to the Winyaw settlement, in the area of Winyaw Bay near present-day Georgetown.

Maurice Moore's visits to the Lower Cape Fear had kindled his interest in its settlement. His effective rout of the Indians made such a settlement possible; and all he lacked was the proper land patents from the Lords Proprietors.

The Lords Proprietors had divided their Carolina gift into three parcels: the Albemarle, named for George Monck, Duke of Albemarle, which was in the north; Clarendon, named for Edward Hyde, the Earl of Clarendon, in the middle; and Craven, honoring William, Lord Craven, south of Cape Romaine. County Clarendon's failure had prompted concentration on Albemarle and Craven, which were enjoying growth. Over the years the Lords Proprietors had formulated a master plan for setting up their proprietary colony. One of the more energetic Proprietors, Sir Anthony Ashley Cooper, Lord Shaftesbury, had had his secretary, John Locke, draft a document called the Fundamental Constitution of Carolina. This constitutional curiosity created a Carolina nobility: a 3,000-acre land grant made a *baron*; 12,000 acres, a *cassique*; and 20,000 acres, a *landgrave*. Settlers, who were the *leetmen*, paid an annual quitrent (a fixed rent paid to their feudal masters) of one-half penny per acre to finance the administration. The first land grant in the Lower Cape

Above: *Pirates who plagued the trade routes in the early 18th century often found refuge in the quiet waters of the sounds behind the outer islands. From a distance a keen eye might detect a topsail and mast flying the dreaded skull and crossbones. The unfurling of the Jolly Roger meant the pirates had arrived. Courtesy, North Carolina State Archives*

Left: *Major Stede Bonnet was the most famous pirate of the Cape Fear. He was captured near present-day Southport by Captain William Rhett of South Carolina and taken to Charleston for trial and execution. The "Gentleman Pirate" was buried below the low tide mark at Charleston's waterfront. Courtesy, North Carolina State Archives*

Right: *Elephant tokens, made of copper in a half-penny denomination, were struck in England in 1694 as an advertising gimmick to interest people in settling the American colonies. Courtesy, North Carolina State Archives*

Fear was granted in 1713 to landgrave Thomas Smith of Charleston; it included modern-day Bald Head Island.

Although the proprietors had officially stopped issuing patents in County Clarendon, George Burrington, the governor of North Carolina appointed by the proprietors, decided it was time to exploit the area's potential. Burrington took it upon himself to spend the winter of 1724-1725 in the wilderness of the Cape Fear. He believed the region should be colonized, but he was the kind of man who would assess the situation personally. In the lonely isolation of the wilderness he sounded the river and streams, noted the great stands of pine, and became increasingly convinced that the Lower Cape Fear offered him and his friends the opportunity for great wealth. When he returned to the Albemarle he began issuing grants—even though he was not empowered to do so—to himself, and a few select friends, who, being men of substance, could transfer their slaves to the banks of the Cape Fear to create a new plantation society in the wilderness. Shortly after the project gained momentum, Burrington was recalled to England and his successor, Sir Richard Everard, took up where he had left off.

A few of the grants went to men of the Albemarle but the majority went to families such as the Moores living in the Goose Creek settlement of South Carolina on an affluent of the Cooper River on the northern outskirts of present-day Charleston, South Carolina. The Goose Creek clan, dominated by the Moore family, had built South Carolina's only Anglican church outside of Charleston and named it St. James. The St. James congregation of Goose Creek had earned a reputation for being clannish, irascible, fiercely Anglican, politically active, and defiant to authority of any kind. Maurice Moore had already determined that settlement of the Cape Fear was desirable and he persuaded his kinsmen and friends of the Goose Creek faction to follow his lead. As a result, many of the founding families of the Lower Cape Fear—by the names of Allen, Dry, Eagles, Grainger, Hasell, Howe, Izard, Moore, Quince, Rhett, Trott, and Wright—along with other South Carolina families by the names of Hyrne, Toomer, and Watters, found their way to the region, bringing with them a tidewater heritage and political temperament that would spawn revolutionaries.

Governor Burrington immediately regretted his choice of grantees, for he was constantly at odds with the Moore family, who had come to dominate the Cape Fear as they had Goose Creek. The Moores traced their zest for resistance to the Irish rebellion, when, as the O'Moores, they had played a major role in the rebellion against the Roundheads. James Moore, who eventually became governor of South Carolina, had come to Charleston from England. He married Margaret Berringer, stepdaughter of County Clarendon governor Sir John Yeamans, and it seems likely that this relationship kindled an interest in the Lower Cape Fear. While the County Clarendon settlement failed, John Moore's four grandsons—James, Maurice, Roger,

Many of the Cape Fear's first settlers came from Goose Creek, South Carolina. It is interesting to note that at both locales settlers built an Anglican church with striking architectural similarities and named each parish St. James. The gravestones found at St. James, Goose Creek, South Carolina (above), and Wilmington, North Carolina (right), also tell the story of a shared heritage. Courtesy, Carolina Art Association

St. James Church (Colonial)

Commenced 1751
Completed 1770
Material for new Church 1839

Presented by CLAYTON GIL.

and Nathaniel—managed to establish a permanent settlement.

Like the Moores, many of the settlement's founding families shared ancestors who had a connection with the Cape Fear's early history. Edward Moseley had once shared a jail cell with Maurice Moore, following a breaking-and-entering escapade while the two were trying to prove that North Carolina governor Charles Eden was in league with Blackbeard. The conversation must have turned to Moore's Indian-fighting adventures along the Cape Fear, for within a few years, Moseley, like Moore, owned large tracts of land in the region. The Rhetts descended from Colonel William Rhett, who had captured the "Gentleman Pirate," Stede Bonnet. The stories of Sir John Yeamans, Moore's Indian fights, and Rhett's round with the pirates were the stories the members of these founding families had heard since infancy. To them, the land of the Cape Fear was more than just land; it represented a legacy of swashbuckling adventure that not even the strong-willed Governor Burrington could wrestle away.

When Burrington returned to the Cape Fear as royal governor in 1731 (after George II had made North Carolina a royal province by purchasing seven of the Lords Proprietors' shares) he discovered that the Moores had solidified their position of power and importance even further. Of the region's 105,000 patented acres, they collectively held 83,000. More than 1,200 people now lived along the Cape Fear, but the majority were black slaves concentrated among a few families. The Goose Creek families had brought their slaves with them, and established a plantation system based on the production of naval stores, wood staves, some rice, and some indigo. Roger Moore had established himself at Orton and Kendall plantations and had become important enough to earn the title "Chief gentleman of all Cape Fear." Baron, Cassique, or Landgrave were titles too trifling for Roger Moore. His tomb at Orton—the region's only surviving Colonial-period plantation—proclaims "Here lies King Roger Moore."

Maurice Moore also built himself a town—Brunswick. The lots were selling well in this first successful development and part of that was due to the fact that Brunswick had been sanctioned as an official Crown port. At the same time, the Crown created New Hanover Precinct. The names Hanover and Brunswick were to honor the German lineage of George II. Brunswick became the official county seat of New Hanover Precinct, and its port was soon bustling with traffic as the majority of new settlers came by ship and carried on their commerce via the Cape Fear River.

The majority of these first settlers—most of whom had come from the Goose Creek area and the Albemarle—did not fit the stereotype of the emigrant. They did not flee persecution or poverty but were well-educated for their time and possessed the material hallmarks of the gentry: featherbeds, pewter, silver, books, portraits, and fine furniture. Most brought slaves to run the house and work

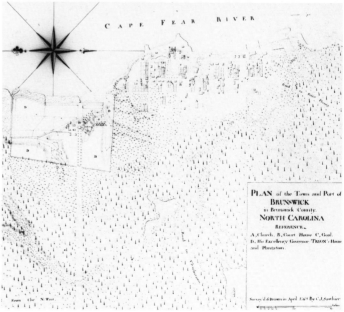

Above: *C.J. Sauthier drew this map of Brunswick in 1769. Forty years earlier the Crown had officially purchased Carolina from the Lords Proprietors, and Brunswick became the county seat of New Hanover Precinct. The port bustled with commerce and the activities of the colonists who came to settle in Brunswick or on plantations along the Cape Fear River and its tributaries. Courtesy, North Carolina State Archives*
Left: *The oldest land grant in the lower Cape Fear was given to Landgrave Thomas Smith of Charleston, South Carolina, in 1713. It included Smith's Island, or Baldhead Island, where an active trading post was run by Smith's representatives. Courtesy, South Carolina Historical Society*

the land. Despite the fact that they were men of property and substance, they believed the land held a promise and that they were equal to the challenge of the wilderness. Anyone who has ever penetrated the backwaters of the Cape Fear needs little imagination to envision the isolation that vast wilderness of the 18th century posed. Hugh Meredith, who had been sent by his business partner, Benjamin Franklin, to write about the frontier, wrote of his 1730 visit:

> Most of the county is well clothed with tall pines, excepting the Swamps, Savannahs, and some Small Strips by the Side of the Rivers. The only town they have as yet is Brunswick . . . having a commodious Place for Ships to lie safe in all Weathers, and is likely to be a Place of Trade, and the seat of Government . . . The River Clarendon [Cape Fear] is esteemed the best for navigation of any along that Shore . . . Here are foxes, wolves, wildcats, possums, raccoons, and panthers always, and bears, sometimes in great plenty, also plenty of deer . . . alligators are very numerous here but not very mischievous; however on their account swimming is less practiis'd here than in the Northern Provinces.

The coat of arms of "His Excellency Gabriel Johnston, Esq." is pictured here. As governor of the colony, Johnston used his influence to transfer the seat of government from Brunswick to Newton, a settlement farther up the river. The governor renamed the town Wilmington after his patron, Spencer Compton, the Earl of Wilmington. From the North Carolina Collection, UNC Library, Chapel Hill

The settlers established their plantations on the high ground overlooking the Cape Fear and Northeast rivers. The land was cleared by chopping down the trees or by ringing the trees so they would die naturally. Undergrowth was chopped out and the Indian method of burning cleared the fields. Slaves did most of the heavy work. Often bricks were made on the premises to build the houses, whose high locations offered lovely views.

Unfortunately, abandonment, fire, decay, and the moist climate have worked together to almost totally destroy the plantation houses of the Lower Cape Fear. Orton's house remains, but the facade seen today is antebellum and the colonial portion of the house has been disguised by renovations. The house at The Hermitage appeared on Cape Fear Bank notes, but it burned in the 19th century. Oakland in Bladen County and Sloop Point (formerly known as Ashe's Neck) at Topsail Sound are the only extant plantation houses. The brick kitchen at Sloop Point has been dated around 1726, which places it as the oldest house on the Southern North Carolina coast. Place names, deeds, and genealogies tell the romantic tales of the plantations of the old Cape Fear. Some carried names which conjured up faraway places, people, and gardens: Belgrange, Belvedere, Belville, Buchoi, Clarendon, The Hermitage, Hilton, Kendall, Lilliput, Mount Gallant, Orton, and York. Others immortalized their owners: Ashe's Neck, Clayton Hall, Dalrymple Place, Davis Plantation, Dobbs Place, Governor's Point, Halton Lodge, Castle Haynes, Howe's Point, Hyrneham, Lillington Hall, Moorefields, Moseley Hall, Rice's Plantation, Russellborough, and Swann Point. Others captured the local ambiance and geographical features of the site: Bowland, Cedar Grove, The Forks, Green Hill, Hullfields, Negro Head Point, The Oaks, Old Town, Old Town Creek, Pleasant Hall, Pleasant Oaks, Rock Hill, Rocky Run, Rose Hill, Springfield, Spring Garden, Stag Park, Strawberry, and the Vats. These plantations earned a reputation for dispensing hospitality. One governor, Josiah Martin, was to call this area "the region of politeness."

Of course, not every new settler could be a member of the established landed gentry with fields to till, forests to harvest, and slaves to do the work. Some, of necessity, needed to have their land in a smaller parcel; Brunswick was a town that made this possible. Brunswick was a model town that was planned, laid out, and developed by Maurice Moore with assistance from his brother Roger. The town was established on a tract donated by Maurice and Nathaniel Moore. There was a town common and 336 half-acre lots. Historian Elizabeth McCoy said that many early lot descriptions could be summarized in "poles and pines": poles marked the length, while pines marked the spot.

Brunswick prospered because of the vast pine forest which surrounded it. In a time when the nation who ruled the sea ruled the world, it was imperative for Great Britain to keep her wooden fleet in peak condition, which was made possible by the use of naval stores—turpentine, pitch, and tar, plus timber. The pines of the Lower Cape Fear provided that yield and for a time the Port of Brunswick was the "Naval Stores Capital of the World." This commerce, plus the fact that Brunswick was the seat of government for the Precinct of New Hanover, made her the leading town in the region—but her geographical location made her vulnerable to attack and storm damage, and her relationship with the Moores made other factions anxious to undermine her strength.

Navigating up the river from Brunswick, one would follow a channel on the western side of the stream. At Old Town Creek silt formed a shoal, which shallowed the channel to a 10-foot depth; but craft with a lesser draft could continue to the Forks at the southern end of Eagles' Island where the Northwest branch and the Northeast branch of the Cape Fear River merged. The broad stream along the north side of Eagles' Island was known as the Thoroughfare. At this site on the east bank of the Cape Fear River, where the anchorage was good and the water was free from destructive seaworms, the town of Wilmington would be built.

James Wimble, a Boston mariner, began selling lots in a town he called Carthage on the east side of the Cape Fear River in 1733. Wimble had purchased the property from John Watson who had obtained the original patent from Governor George Burrington. Watson had also sold land to Michael Higgins and Joshua Grainger, Sr. For a while the town was called New Liverpool (probably because of Wimble's familiarity with Liverpool, England) and then the name was changed to Newton ("new town") to distinguish it from the old town of Brunswick. Land sales soared. Wimble had a map drawn of his new town on which a turreted castle, labeled Wimbleton Castle, appears. It has never been determined whether this was a castle of fact or imagination. While no street bears its developer's name, Castle Street remains as a reminder of Wimble's grandiose plans.

Gabriel Johnston was the governor who put the events in motion that culminated in the formation of a place named Wilmington. When he arrived in 1734, he inherited Governor Burrington's feud with the Moores. The Moores not only were the great landowners, but because of their impressive connections through marriage and their prolific family (George sired 28 children) they were numerous and powerful. As a result, the family had won many a skirmish, but in the end Johnston would win the war. Johnston, like Burrington, had a temper, but he was a more adroit manipulator. After assessing the situation, Johnston determined to cast his fortunes with the Wimble group by purchasing property adjacent to theirs. He was well aware that a town is much more than a collection of buildings, so he used his gubernatorial power to support measures that would transfer the county seat from Brunswick to Newton. By 1739, he had progressed to the stage where Colonel William Bartram of Bladen County could introduce legislation establishing the town and township of Wilmington. Johnston had selected the name Wilmington to flatter his patron, Spencer Compton, the Earl of Wilmington. In February 1740, the town was officially incorporated by an act of the North Carolina General Assembly.

Slowly but surely Wilmington gained importance while Brunswick lost ground. A courthouse was erected which enabled Johnston to have the Court of the Exchequer and the Court of the Oyer and Terminer transferred from Brunswick. Johnston, a Highland Scot, also encouraged his friends to emigrate so that his coterie of Highland Scots strengthened. It is estimated that by the late 18th century over 20,000 Scots had emigrated to the Cape Fear Valley.

Once Wilmington was on the map, it did not take long for her to be discovered. Hugh Meredith's accounts of the Cape Fear, which had appeared in the Pennsylvania Gazette, stimulated Pennsylvanians to come. The town layout had streets reminiscent of Philadelphia, but both cities seem to be indebted to Liverpool, England for many of its street names. Individuals continued to come from Bar-

bados and England. Some Irish and Welsh came in the 1730s with Pennsylvania Germans arriving in the 1750s and 1760s. The majority of white settlers shared a common heritage of the English language.

The *Wilmington Town Book* gives a good picture of life in early Wilmington. Wilmington was founded because it made a good port and its river linked it to the sea. The early residents' maritime heritage is reflected in their occupations: mariner, shipbuilder, merchant, ship's captain, pilot, chandler, cooper, cordswain, seaman, portmaster, customs officer, quarantine officer. Laws were passed to keep the peace and punishments were devised to keep lawbreakers in check. Colonial Wilmington had a jail, a pillory, stocks, a dunking stool, and gallows. Laws were enacted to regulate lots and building, to enact fire controls and price controls, and to ensure honesty in selling goods. Despite the river at the foot of Market, the wells that gushed forth, and the streams that meandered through the town, fire was a constant threat and the history of Wilmington includes a long list of tremendous blazes. Chimney fires were commonplace and residents were required to sweep their chimneys regularly and to own leather

Important in the naval stores industry was this tool called a hack. It was used to gouge the trunk of a pine tree so the rosin could run into a box or cup to be collected at a later date. Photo by Freda Wilkins. Courtesy, New Hanover County Museum

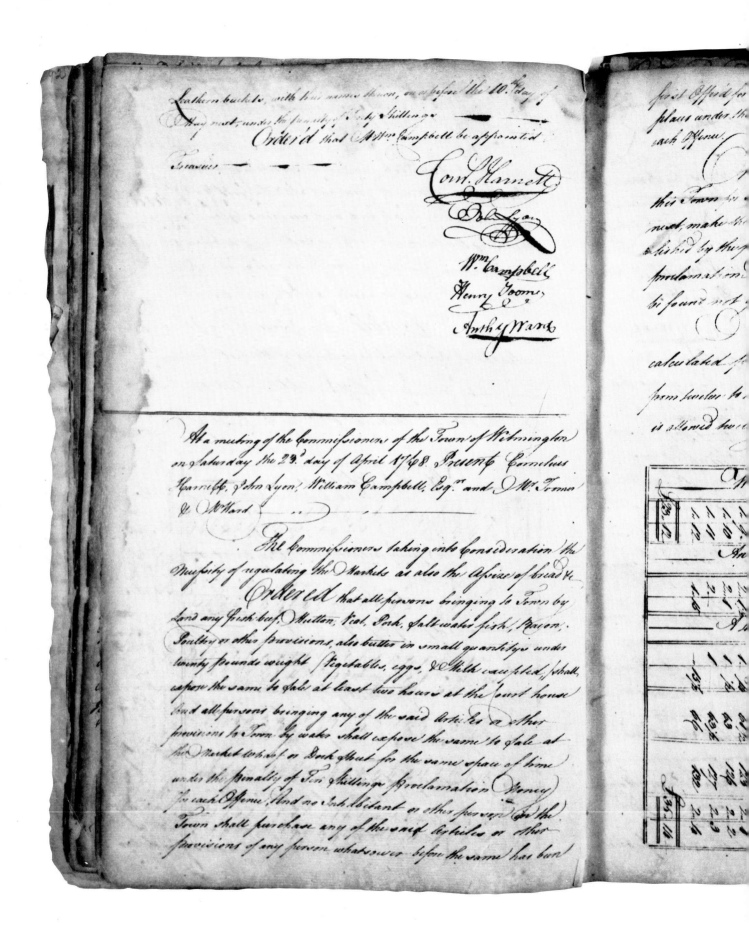

Leathern buckets, with their names thereon, on or before the 10th day of May next, under the penalty of Forty Shillings. —— Order'd that Mr. Campbell be appointed Treasurer ——

Corn. Harnett
Jno. Lyon
Wm. Campbell
Henry Toomer
Anthy Ward

At a meeting of the Commissioners of the Town of Wilmington on Saturday the 23d day of April 1768. Present Cornelius Harnett, John Lyon, William Campbell, Esqr. and Mr. Toomer & Mr. Ward

The Commissioners taking into Consideration the Necessity of regulating the Markets as also the Assize of bread &c.

Order'd that all persons bringing to Town by Land any fresh beef, Mutton, Veal, Pork, Saltwater fish, Bacon, Poultry or other provisions, also butter in small quantitys under twenty pounds weight (Vegetables, eggs, & Milk excepted,) shall expose the same to sale at least two hours at the Court house but all persons bringing any of the said Articles or other provisions to Town by water shall expose the same to sale at the Market wharf or Dock street for the same space of time under the penalty of Ten Shillings proclamation Money for each Offence, And no Inch. Abitant or other person (in the Town shall purchase any of the said Articles or other provisions of any person whatsoever before the same has been

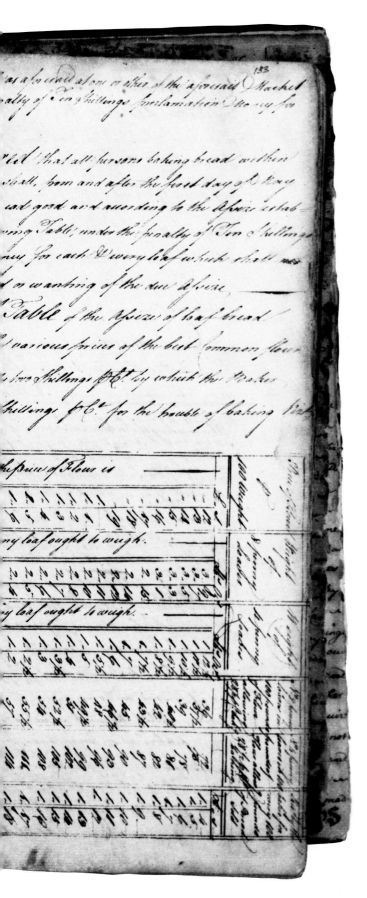

fire buckets to be used in the bucket brigade. In 1775 the town bought its first of many fire engines.

Although the white population was in the majority in town, the overall population of the area residents showed a heavier concentration of blacks than whites. Of the 2,005 taxable residents listed in New Hanover County in 1765, 529 were white and 1,476 were black. This uneven ratio struck fear into the hearts of the white minority who were constantly on guard against slave uprisings. As a result, many of the town's first laws were designed to control the movement of slaves. Some slaves had become freedmen and they were required to wear identifying badges and to observe the curfews.

In 1743, the freeholders (property owners) of Wilmington elected James Campbell, Rufus Marsden, Richard Hellier, James Smallwood, and Dr. Armand deRosset as town commissioners. Two of these men were merchants, as were many of Wilmington's first citizens. Men of property often referred to themselves as "planter" when listing their occupations, as this reference was preferable to listing their professional standing. To be a planter implied that one owned a plantation, which had great social distinction. Marmaduke Jones called himself "Attorney and Gentleman."

Class distinctions were known; yet there was easy fraternizing at the courthouse and at the markethouse. For a fledgling small town, Wilmington could boast of a high ratio of well-born, well-educated, propertied citizens. At least 24 physicians practiced in Wilmington prior to 1778, among them North Carolina's first M.D., Armand deRosset. There were also a good number of attorneys; but because their licensing could be revoked by the governor if they were out of favor, they were sometimes out of practice. This happened to Samuel Swann and Edward Moseley. Men of the law from Wilmington held important offices in colonial North Carolina. Some of these included Samuel Swann, Eleazer Allen, John Baptisa Ashe, John Ashe, Samuel Ashe, James Hasell, Martin Howard, Joseph Anderson, Thomas Child, George Nicholas, and Marmaduke Jones.

The colonial clique of local aristocrats who could afford more oppulent lifestyles often exchanged books as well as ideas. John Eustace, a physician, was described as a man "who united wit, genius, and learning." His will listed a library inventory of over 292 books. He had been a correspondent with Laurence Sterne, author of *Tristram Shandy*, and it has always been tantalizing to the historian with a literary bent to wonder if Greenville Sound's Shandy Hall and Toby Hall relate to this correspondence. John Fergus, another doctor, was described as "Of stately presence, with velvet coat, cocked hat

The Wilmington Town Book, in which were recorded transactions of the government, gives us an insight into town life in the period from 1743-1778. To regulate the food markets and the sale of bread was part of the commissioners' duty. The "Table of Assize of Loaf Bread" was a handy guide to assure uniformity. Courtesy, State Department of Archives and History, Raleigh

and gold headed cane, a graduate of Edinburgh, and an excellent Greek and Latin scholar.''

Since North Carolina was a crown colony, it was expected to support its king in his military campaigns. During King George's War more than a hundred Cape Fear men enlisted. Captain James Innes, a Wilmingtonian who spoke Spanish, was made commander of a North Carolina company. The war's most deadly engagement took place in April 1741 at Cartagena, New Granada (Columbia). The American colonists fighting in their king's behalf anticipated an easy victory; instead it was a rout. Many were killed or wounded and tropical fever took its toll among those who survived the attack. When the men of Cape Fear sailed home, their numbers had been reduced to 25.

Although the Seven Years' (French and Indian) War's theater of battle was too far removed geographically to have much effect on the Lower Cape Fear, it did provide an opportunity for some of its citizens to earn military distinction. Among these soldiers were James Innes, Thomas McManus, James Moore, and Hugh Waddell, who served as officers; both Innes and Waddell were hailed as heroes.

In 1754, North Carolina was required to raise a regiment and Colonel James Innes of Cartagena renown was placed in command. Despite his youth, he had merited authority because of his proven capability. George Washington was under Innes' command and he wrote of his superior: "I rejoice that I am likely to be happy under

Spencer Compton, the Earl of Wilmington, was influential in securing Gabriel Johnston's appointment as governor. Compton later became Prime Minister of England. Courtesy, New Hanover County Museum

James Murray was one of the most affluent and influential members of Governor Gabriel Johnston's Scotch Highlander coterie. Many members of this group fled the Cape Fear during the American Revolution because of their allegiance to the Loyalist cause. Courtesy, Donald Lennon

the command of an experienced officer, and a man of sense."

Two years later North Carolina was required to provide another regiment and Wilmington newcomer Hugh Waddell went off with this group. During the campaign to capture Fort Duquesne in which Waddell commanded North Carolina's forces, he met a young gentleman poet from Philadelphia named Thomas Godfrey. Waddell and Godfrey became comrades of intellect as well as arms, and when their military duties were over, Godfrey accompanied Waddell to Wilmington for a reunion with his North Carolina friends.

While visiting Masonborough, the plantation home of Caleb Grainger, Godfrey wrote a play, The *Prince of Parthia*, which was later produced in Philadelphia and earned Godfrey a place in theatrical annals as the author of the first play written and produced in America. Godfrey died shortly after writing the play, but his works were preserved by his friends, who made them a treasured part of the collection of the new Cape Fear Library which they had established.

In 1760 Wilmington obtained borough status with a flourish of Governor Arthur Dobbs' pen. John Sampson was elected the borough's first mayor. His Honor could take more than mere parochial pride in Wilmington. In a little more than two decades, a wilderness had been turned into a thriving port. Ships crowded the wharves and the town prospered, while the pines still seemed to reach to infinity and the river still led to the sea.

◆ ◆ ◆

In 1760 Governor Arthur Dobbs bestowed borough status on Wilmington. The charter he signed conveyed the traditional privileges of an English borough, including the right to hold markets, fairs, and courts. It also provided for a government that presided over an area extending within two and one-half miles of the courthouse. Courtesy, Lower Cape Fear Historical Society. Gift of Mr. Henry J. MacMillan

In the French and Indian War Brigadier General Hugh Waddell of Wilmington (pictured here) commanded North Carolina's forces in the capture of Fort Duquesne. During the campaign he met Thomas Godfrey and persuaded the poet to visit him in Wilmington. Courtesy, Lower Cape Fear Historical Society

Pathways of Patriarchs:

A chill wind off the Cape Fear River snapped the flags strung from the ships crowding the Wilmington Harbor that Saturday, February 7, 1761. The day before Governor Arthur Dobbs had proclaimed George III to be king in the presence of the members of council, the prominent planters, and principal inhabitants of Brunswick. On Saturday the celebration moved to Wilmington where the formalities were repeated. The militia marched; a triple 21-gun salute startled gulls from their perches. The assembled citizens answered the echoing retorts with loud huzzas. Such an auspicious day called for toasts all around. Ordinaries ran low on grog and rum, rich men brought out their decanters of Madeira and French brandy while their ladies unlocked the punch and syllabub supplies, and the poorer folk made do with hard cider and persimmon beer. It was a date to remember. Governor Dobbs wrote to London:

> The evening concluded by bonfires, illuminations, and a ball and supper with all unanimity and demonstrations of joy.

No official record exists to relate whether the new sovereign knew or cared how his colonial subjects of New Hanover County, North Carolina, celebrated his ascension to the throne. No doubt their provincial festivities paled in comparison to London's brilliant pageantry, but their enthusiasm was genuine. Only the chill salty breeze portended the bitter political storm that lay ahead.

Nature's storm struck the shore in September 1761. The autumnal equinox's gales began Saturday the 20th and a howling hurricane battered Cape Fear on the 23rd. Every ship but one was torn from her anchorage and driven to Brunswick's shore. Shorn roofs flew off with the wind, houses toppled, trees fell, and the driving rain poured into every chink. At the height of the storm's fury, the sea broke through to form a new inlet a little below Brunswick. When the new channel was sounded it was found to have a depth of 18 feet and a girth of half a mile. In those days, before hurricanes were given names, the great storm was simply known as the hurricane that formed New Inlet.

A storm of the tempest-in-the-teapot variety swirled through the Cape Fear the following autumn. The wags declared that propriety had taken a holiday when Governor Arthur Dobbs announced that he intended to marry Justina Davis. The groom was 73, the bride 15, which provided grist for the lampooner's mill. As the fresh young bride stood before the congregation at Brunswick's St. Phillips to take her vows she could little imagine the momentous changes that lay before her, her groom, the English Crown, or Brunswick itself. Dobbs would die in her arms two years hence, his remains to be placed not far from the place she now stood; Russellborough, the royal governor's home, would be destroyed in the war between the colonists and the mother country; Justina herself would marry another governor, Abner Nash; and Brunswick and St. Phillips would both be burned in the Revolutionary War. Only

the ruins of the majestic St. Phillips would remain; the empty vaulted windows would frame a pine wilderness encroaching upon a time and place that once had been.

A printer named Andrew Steuart settled in Wilmington in 1764. He brought along a printing press and soon began publishing the *North Carolina Gazette.* Poor transportation insured that all news was old news, but those lucky enough to be literate were delighted to have a local paper to bring word from England, Europe, and the other colonies as well as provincial news.

The town the *Gazette* served in 1765 was considered the colony's leading metropolis, although some visitors found it wanting, such as the night owl Peter DuBois who complained: "I cannot yet find social company who will drink claret and smoke tobacco til four in the morning." Yet the severest critic could not deny that Wilmington was growing. One visitor estimated that the town held 200 houses. Some were of wood that was bare or whitewashed, but DuBois reckoned that "many [were] of brick, two, and three stories high with double piazzas which make a good appearance." (One house of the period that survives is the Smith-Anderson house at 102 Orange Street.) Dressed ballast stones had been used to build a few walls, and picket fences enclosed some gardens, but Wilmington still had a rural character as chickens, geese, pigs, goats, cows, and horses roamed the sandy or muddy streets at will. One observer sneered that Wilmington was "nothing better than a village," while another termed it "the most flourishing town in the province," and yet another, "the principal trading town in [the] province."

One had only to look to the river to see evidence of trade. Ships of varied shapes and sizes crowded the waterfront wharves. At the southern extremity of the harbor stood a great cypress garlanded with moss. This tree was known as the Dram Tree, for it was at that spot seamen paused from their duties to take a dram before hoisting the sails into full canvas. Ship traffic made life exciting in the port town. Even small boys perched upon the bank could determine—by mast, rigging, sails, and flag—each ship's destination, cargo and business. From the West Indies came the brig, or brigantine, with her two masts and square sails. She could carry 100 tons and with easy modification be adapted for privateering. The schooners and sloops plied the coastal trade. Square-rigged, three-masted ships made the treacherous New England run or weathered the Atlantic crossing, bringing exports of the British Isles—brass, books, cards, china, furniture, hardware, nails, newspapers, toys, wine—and more colonists. The drougher, a type of barge used in the West Indies, cast a low silhouette along the river, and the lowly hollowed-out log perriaugers and cypress canoes skimmed along with astonishing speed.

The bulk of Wilmington's export trade was derived from the Cape Fear's trees. In 1765 the area boasted over 55 sawmills. Dammed creek and branch streams were harnessed to propel the massive millstones that powered the vertical cutting saws to cut the heartwood of pitch pine and oak into planks. The forest yielded over three mil-

John Burgwin, one of Cape Fear's most successful citizens, was at the same time planter, shipbuilder, merchant, and civic leader. He was also the builder of one of Wilmington's well known landmarks: the Burgwin-Wright House. This portrait by Copley now hangs in the Kennedy Gallery. Courtesy, Lower Cape Fear Historical Society

lion feet of lumber a year. Cypress shingles and oak staves were also hewn for export. Local coopers turned the staves into barrels to hold the turpentine, tar, and pitch—the pines' bonus dividends.

Slaves were imported from the West Indies to labor in the naval stores industry. They felled the trees, boxed and tapped the pines for the resin that would be distilled into turpentine, stoked the kiln fires with lightwood to bake the resin into tar, and stirred the iron cauldrons in which three barrels of tar were boiled down to two barrels of pitch.

Slaves also worked the fields to reap the Lower Cape Fear's money crop of rice. Rice cultivation and harvesting demanded long hours of bending in the sun while mosquitoes swarmed and the stench from the putrid water permeated the air. As the rice season progressed, the slaves hoed the soil, planted the seed, sickled the crop, winnowed and flailed the rice for threshing, and hand-polished the grains with mortar and pestle. For a brief time, slaves tilled hemp and indigo fields and cultivated tender mulberries to feed silkworms, but these industries proved more lucrative in theory than in practice.

Because of the labor needs of the naval stores and rice fields, the Lower Cape Fear counted a 67% black population in 1767. This heavy density of slaves set the Lower Cape Fear apart from the western part of North Carolina where slaves were few. It has been estimated that the majority of these slaves were owned by a small group of about 20 Cape Fear planters, some of whom maintained residences within Wilmington.

Not all slaves worked the plantations. Some were craftsmen and laborers who lived in town. Records also show that a few were river pilots. A minute proportion were freedmen but laws were enacted to control the whereabouts of all blacks to ward off potential insurrections. But some slaves tried to escape their bondage. Tunnelways under the streets that lead to the river have been used for a wide variety of illicit undertakings in Wilmington's history, including the means for escape for runaway slaves. Sometimes slaves did organize. The New Hanover County Court of 1767 reported: "Upwards of 20 runaway Slaves in a body Arm'd were at large." The sheriff and a posse of 30 went after them. Some runaways came to a sorry end, such as London, a slave owned by the Honorable Lewis Henry deRosset. The 1766 New Hanover Court record states that London "ran away and was outlawed, upon being taken up, jumped into the river and drowned himself."

A distinctive ethnic feature of the town was the number of Scottish and Scotch-Irish merchants who were the entrepreneurs of successful businesses. This concentration of an enterprising, hard-working mercantile class had a positive influence on Wilmington's development. Shoppers came to Wilmington from the hinterlands and neighboring plantations by foot, horseback, post chaise, coach, or boat. Roads ran from Wilmington to Bath and Edenton, and the Brunswick Road led to South Carolina. River transportation ranged from lowly homemade canoes to elaborate barges rowed by liveried slaves.

The Cape Fear's most successful colonial planter, shipowner, merchant, and gentleman was an Englishman named John Burgwin (1731-1803). A handsome portrait by John Singleton Copley, an impressive townhouse, and his plantation, The Hermitage, all document his attractiveness, taste, and importance. The 21-year-old alumnus of Eton and Oxford arrived in Wilmington in 1752. His youth, prospects, and charming demeanor provided him an easy entree into Wilmington's society, and he soon became engaged to one of the Lower Cape Fear's most eligible spinsters, Margaret Haynes, daughter of Captain Roger Haynes. She brought to her husband the property adjoining Castle Haynes, and it was on that property that John Burgwin built the Georgian mansion he named The Hermitage.

John Burgwin succeeded in business; his five ships traded along the coast, as well as with Barbados, London, and Amsterdam. His rising fortunes ran parallel with his civic responsibilities; he served as Governor Dobbs' private secretary, as clerk of the New Hanover County Superior Court, and as treasurer of the Province of North Carolina.

Around 1770 he began building the handsome townhouse at Third and Market known in Wilmington as the Burgwin-Wright house. It is not known how much time he spent there, as his wife died in 1770, and an accident resulting in a severely broken leg required him to spend a long convalescence at The Hermitage.

He went to England in 1775 to seek help for his poorly mended leg, but because he was a man of property who traveled to England during the Revolutionary War, many assumed he was a Tory. While he was there, the newly declared state of North Carolina confiscated his property. When Burgwin returned to America to extradite his property and interests, he brought with him a young woman, Elizabeth Bush, with whom he had fallen in love in England. He successfully petitioned the North Carolina Assembly to return his property to him, thus ending the suspicions that he was a Tory.

When Burgwin brought Elizabeth back to the Carolinas as his bride in 1782, she delivered a daughter, Eliza, on her first night in America. But Elizabeth proved too frail for motherhood and the country, and she died after the birth of a third child, leaving a grieving husband at the plantation so aptly named for a man who had buried two young wives. The townhouse was sold to Judge Joshua Grainger Wright, and Burgwin made his home at The Hermitage until his death in 1803.

Burgwin, like many others, must have read with more than cursory interest the August 10, 1764 *North Carolina Magazine* which reported:

> We hear from Cape Fear, that a Lieutenant-Governor of this Province is appointed at home, one Colonel Tryan [sic], an Officer in the Guards; and that he is expected out immediately.... The good people of Wilmington engaged a large house in Wilmington for the reception and accommodation of the governor on his arrival in the Province, upon a certainty that he will settle among them there.

(Wilmingtonians had become accustomed to their governor living in the Lower Cape Fear, a fact resented by the citizens of New Bern.) When Tryon, along with his wife and three-year-old daughter, arrived at the Cape Fear aboard the *Friendship* to take up residence at Russellborough—the 55-acre plantation on the Orton tract which had served as home to Governor Dobbs—it was in full anticipation that the aging and ailing Dobbs would be anxious to be relieved. Tryon went ashore at Brunswick to discover that the Dobbs' had no intention of leaving before spring and that the Tryons had no place to stay other than the ship. They lived in temporary quarters until Dobbs died in March 1765.

On October 24, 1764, Tryon officially assumed office, and

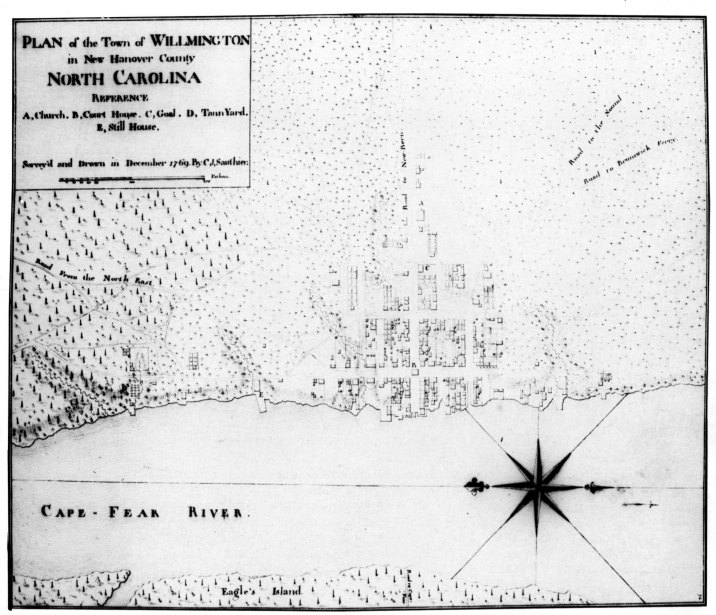

PLAN of the Town of WILLMINGTON
in New Hanover County
NORTH CAROLINA
REFERENCE
A, Church. B, Court House. C, Goal. D, Tann Yard.
E, Still House.

Survey'd and Drawn in December 1769. By C.J. Sauthier.

Road to the Sound

Road to Brunswick Ferry

Road to New Bern

Road from the North East

CAPE - FEAR RIVER.

Eagle's Island.

Just below the forks of the river, across from Eagles' Island on the river's eastern bank, the town of Wilmington emerged. This 1769 map shows how the village had grown in the 36 years since its founding. We see a church, courthouse, goal (jail), as well as many private residences. Courtesy, North Carolina State Archives. From the original in the Library, British Museum, London

On October 25, 1760, when his grandfather died, George, Prince of Wales, became George III, King of England. He wanted to be a good king and a father to his people, and was very upset when his children in the American colonies objected vehemently to a little discipline. From the North Carolina Collection, UNC Library, Chapel Hill

quickly endeavored to acquaint himself with his province. At every stopping place he learned of the colonists' dissatisfaction with the Stamp Act, a tax which was regarded as unfair, and which was bound to place economic hardships on the colony.

From the outset of his governorship, Tryon was confronted with difficult decisions. He had been appointed to rule a people who had established a tradition of anti-authoritarian attitudes and a fierce love of liberty. When the British Parliament passed the Stamp Act, which would become effective November 1, 1765, it in effect threw down a gauntlet to the people of the Lower Cape Fear. The act provided for duties to be paid in cash on all posted items, newspapers, and legal documents including ship clearances, the proceeds to be spent to support British troops stationed in America. Those who did not comply with the act could be tried without jury by the Admiralty Court in Halifax, Nova Scotia.

After the details of the Stamp Act became known, it was obvious that for people whose economy was linked to shipping such measures would be devastating. Judge Maurice Moore wrote a 16-page pamphlet titled "Justice and the Policy of Taxing the American Colonies in Great Britain Considered." His tract showcased his grasp of constitutional law and logic and made it clear that Parliament did not have the right to levy the tax. But Parliament ignored Moore's arguments and the local citizens' anger was so aroused after passage of the Stamp Act that the men of Wilmington organized into the Sons of Liberty to make their displeasure known.

Around 500 men gathered to hang an effigy of Lord Bute, the man they credited with sponsoring the odious Stamp Act. Impassioned toasts were made to "Liberty, Property, and No Stamp Duty." The crowd rounded up *Gazette* publisher Andrew Steuart and directed him not to print the newspaper on stamped paper and to print all the news of the Stamp Act opposition.

Governor Tryon appointed a Duplin County surgeon, Dr. William Houston, to be the stamp collector. When Houston arrived in Wilmington to transact some personal business he quickly discovered that his appointment had caused a furor. A hostile crowd, which included Mayor Frederick Gregg, Alderman Moses deRosset and many seamen, gathered around him. Houston remembered of the confrontation:

> The inhabitants immediately assembled about me and demanded a categorical answer whether I intended to put the Act relating [to] the Stamps in force. The town bell was rung, drums beating, colors flying and a great concourse of people were gathered together.

The doctor's answer was an on-the-spot resignation. Tryon, in an attempt to mollify the local leaders, invited them to Russellborough for a lavish meal. His tactic failed and when H.M.S. *Diligence* arrived on November 28th, there was no official to receive the papers. The official Stamp Collector, who should have made the collections on behalf of the Crown, had resigned, and no one was willing to take his place. Trade ended, and the ports of Brunswick and Wilmington stagnated. Tensions increased as the months passed and the effects of the trade standstill were felt on the local economy.

In mid-January, three ships without the proper stamps were seized by the English as they entered the Cape Fear River near Brunswick; it was ruled they were in violation of the Stamp Act and

The slaves brought to the Carolinas from the West Indies in the 18th century used the same method of planting rice as these women, photographed about 1910. Rice cultivation was introduced to the Cape Fear by planters from the Goose Creek section of South Carolina. The rice they

preferred, Carolina Gold, was sowed first in mid-March by workers using a
gourd with a small hole drilled in the neck. No fertilizer was used, but
growth was controlled by alternate flooding and draining of the fields.
Courtesy, New Hanover County Museum

were to be prosecuted. This ruling so incensed the Sons of Liberty that on February 19, 1766, 1,000 armed men—including planters, aldermen, shipmasters, and citizens of Brunswick, Bladen, New Hanover, and Duplin counties—marched to Governor Tryon's residence at Russellborough and presented a petition of grievances. Tryon ordered the ships released and the crowd dispersed.

In the meantime William Pennington, comptroller of customs, had come to Russellborough to seek sanctuary with the governor. On February 21, Colonel James Moore knocked at Tryon's door and demanded that Pennington come forth. The request was denied and between 400 and 500 men closed in on Russellborough, with Cornelius Harnett at the head of the crowd. Pennington was coerced into resigning and left with Harnett. Pennington was then led to Brunswick where he—along with the Port Collector, William Dry—was pressed into swearing an oath that he would never directly or indirectly issue any stamped paper in North Carolina.

Thus the men of the Cape Fear had successfully waged the American colonies' first open and armed resistance to the Stamp Act. Their forceful actions preceded the Boston Tea Party by almost a decade. When Boston's port was embargoed, the people of the Cape Fear demonstrated their support by sending 300 barrels of provisions; and when the Stamp Act was revoked they could take pride that their resistance had helped to bring it about.

The 43-year-old man who had led the opposition to Governor Tryon was destined to be labeled "The Pride of the Cape Fear" because of his leadership in the revolutionary cause. Cornelius Harnett, Jr. (1723-1781) had spent a lifetime in preparation for that cause. Harnett's father was no stranger to political confrontation. The Harnett house was always awash in political turmoil, and despite successful land speculation, old man Harnett was often in debt. Regular income came from the ferry and the tavern-inn at the ferrylanding at Brunswick.

The tavern's fireside was a meeting place for travelers from across the sea and from the colonies' leading towns. The young Harnett could linger in the tavern's shadows and, as the clay pipe smoke wreathed the rafters and the toddies were consumed, listen to the latest adventure of a traveler from Charleston, Boston, Amsterdam, Barbados, or London. Always he was surrounded by the descendants of the Goose Creek men who told and retold of how their ancestors kept the upper hand with colonial governors.

His first political participation took place at age 25 when the Spanish privateers attacked Brunswick. Harnett responded to the alarm and came forth to help run off the looters. Perhaps that attack upon Brunswick convinced Harnett that the future lay with Wilmington, for two years later he moved to Wilmington, determined to make his fortune. When Wilmington became a borough in 1760 Cornelius Harnett served as alderman. From 1754 to 1775 he served as a representative to the provincial assembly. His oratory came as naturally as his Irish gift of gab, and his aggressive opposition to the Stamp Act made him a natural to become the head of the Sons of Liberty.

In 1773 Josiah Quincy, Jr. of Massachussets came to the Lower Cape Fear to see if there might be support for the revolutionary movement that was growing in New England. Quincy was quick to recognize Harnett's potential for leadership as well as his commitment to the revolutionary cause. The Bostonian gave Harnett the greatest compliment within his frame of reference when he called Harnett "the Samuel Adams of North Carolina." He suggested that Harnett form a North Carolina chapter of the Committee of Correspondence in order to have contact with those of similar political persuasiion and to share intelligence of British activities affecting the colonists.

Harnett did implement a Committee of Correspondence, and served on the Wilmington-New Hanover Safety Committee, formed in 1774 to support the First Continental Congress in Philadelphia.

The repeal of the Stamp Act had provided a lull in the turbulent relations with Great Britain, but the Townsend Acts and Tea Act had put the colonists and the mother country right back on a collision course. The local safety committees orchestrated many of the colonies' responses, and implemented regulations passed by the Continental Congress. A ban had been placed on all imports from Great Britain. In addition, the colonists were to adopt a frugal lifestyle with a cessation of amusements and "expensive entertainments and diversions" including horse racing, dancing, and billiards. Citizens were required by the Wilmington Committee of Safety to "sign the Association," that is, to declare their loyalty to the Revolutionary cause by endorsing the Articles of Association that had been passed by the Continental Congress.

Cornelius Harnett vigorously supported the "Association" and had no difficulty twisting the arms of those less enthusiastic. Since Brunswick and Wilmington's economy was so dependent upon trade, the Association's demands created great personal hardship but the people of the Lower Cape Fear complied.

Since the Stamp Act confrontation at Russellborough, Cornelius Harnett and the other Whig leaders of the Lower Cape Fear had confined their opposition to the Crown to rhetoric rather than physical action, but by June 1775 Governor Josiah Martin had heard rumors that his safety was in jeopardy and fled to Fort Johnston at the mouth of the Cape Fear.

The fort was the physical embodiment of the British presence—that royal authority which had fanned the smoldering embers of revolution for the last decade. The men of the Lower Cape Fear defiantly marched toward a historic rendezvous with Crown authority, and once again Cornelius Harnett, along with future Provincial Congressman John Ashe, and Robert Howe, led the way. Three hundred followers set torches to the symbol of the British Crown. While the flames crackled, Governor Martin fled to the safety of the British warship *Cruzier*, anchored off present-day Southport, thus ending the period of royal rule in North Carolina. Harnett's visible leadership in the demonstration had guaranteed him a place on the British list of most hated enemies of the King.

Harnett's every minute was not spent in fiery demonstrations or giving eloquent orations. Some of the time he attended to the business of making a living, which included the ownership and operation of a successful rum distillery and the operation of boats bringing molasses from the West Indies. He also took time to enjoy the companionship and love of his wife, Mary, and to revel in the pleasures of home life at Maynard, his home on the river just northeast of Wilmington. There he entertained many a traveler and conducted the business of the Wilmington Committee of Safety and Sons of Liberty into the wee hours. Harnett's pleasure in his home life was genuine and his many journeys away from home in the business of the patriotic cause took a toll.

It was Harnett's honor to read aloud to the crowd at Halifax the Declaration of Independence when it arrived August 1, 1776. After he finished reading the stirring proclamation, the dignified Harnett suddenly found himself being lifted up and passed from shoulder to shoulder and carried around the square at the head of a triumphant procession. The next year found him in Philadelphia where he represented North Carolina in the Continental Congress. He found his task burdensome, as he yearned for his family, suffered with painful gout, and grew restless with the long petty wrangling over sectional interests. Finally in 1780 Harnett took "the most fatiguing and disagreeable journey any old fellow [he was 57] ever took" to return home to find that his political dedication had brought many hardships to his loved ones. A large portion of his personal estate was gone, his business was a shambles, and his enemy list was long.

The British had placed Harnett on their most wanted list, and finally found him while he was on yet another patriotic mission, this time to purchase supplies for the revolutionary forces. He was bound at the hands and feet and tossed "like a sack of meal" across a horse's back to be brought into Wilmington as a trophy of war. He was incarcerated in a roofless blockhouse. His poor health and exposure took their toll and although he was finally released, he died in April 1781. While the British thought they had destroyed this man they only succeeded in enshrining him in the memories of the Cape Fear's citizens. North Carolina Historical Highway Marker Number 1 is assigned to this patriot. Its legend simply states:

"D-1 CORNELIUS HARNETT (1723?-1781) — LEADING REVOLUTIONARY STATESMAN."

Harnett was buried in St. James church's graveyard.

From late 1774 to the eve of the Revolution in 1776, the Sons of Liberty, the New Hanover Safety Committee, newspaper editorials, and the militia all worked together to popularize the Whig philosophy; but the town of Wilmington still had its Loyalists, many of them of Scottish descent.

The Scots connection was very strong when the heroine of the Jacobite Rebellion, Flora MacDonald, arrived in the Lower Cape Fear en route to Cross Creek where her husband's relatives had emigrated. Flora had helped Bonnie Prince Charlie escape after the Stuart cause was lost at the Battle of Culloden. Her valor had earned her a place in the ballads, songs, and poetry of Scotland and she was a celebrity wherever she went. In Wilmington she was treated well and a reception was held in her honor; she seemed favorably impressed by Wilmington, although she would become embittered when her husband and his clansmen were defeated by Whig forces on the bridge at Widow Moore's Creek.

Another visitor to the Cape Fear, one "Lady" Susannah Carolina Matilda, made a spectacular impression on Wilmington, although the details of her dubious background would not be discovered until later. Lady Susannah swept into town in November 1771. Her dazzling jewels and smart clothes made it obvious she was someone special and it was not long until she confided that she was the sister of George III, traveling incognito. Word of her royal identity made the rounds and she was feted around town. Not long into her visit she made some discreet inquiries about borrowing money

while waiting for her ship to come in. She was given money by people identified in Louis T. Moore's stories of the Cape Fear region as "fascination-blinded youth" — and then abruptly vanished, leaving the young Wilmingtonians red-faced over their gullibility.

Sarah Wilson, the "Royal Imposter," had indeed acquired her wardrobe and jewels from court; she had stolen them from the queen while in her employ as a serving maid. There she had also developed her excellent imitation of an aristocratic voice and manner. In England she had been tried and sentenced to death, but the queen intervened and the sentence was lightened to deportation to the colonies. She was purchased as a convict in Frederick County, Maryland, but escaped to Virginia, and then to Wilmington where she played her masquerade successfully. She was later found out and "punished" in Charleston, South Carolina.

Another colorful visitor to the region in the days before the Revolution was a Scot and self-proclaimed "lady of quality" named Janet Schaw — who counted among her possessions the "Three P's: Prejudices, Pen, and Paper." Historians are grateful for the latter two items, for Miss Schaw's diligence in writing down her keen observations provides an eyewitness account — albeit jaundiced by a strong Loyalist bias — of a region on the threshold of revolution.

Her prejudices were typical of her class and nationality. She arrived to find the Lower Cape Fear in turmoil. News of the battle of Concord — the legendary shot heard round the world — had strengthened Whig sentiment. Miss Schaw was barely ashore before she became entangled in the political melee. She wrote of Richard Quince, owner of the ship that had brought her to Brunswick:

He . . . is deeply engaged in the new system of politics, in which they all are, more or less, tho Mr. Dry, the collector of customs, is the most zealous and talks treason by the hour.

Miss Schaw had come to the Cape Fear to visit her brother, a successful merchant and master of Schawfield Plantation. As she traveled throughout the region her intellectual curiosity was stimulated by one novel experience after another. She absorbed each new impression with gusto and wrote out her evaluations. Spanish moss, bayberry, cotton, alligators, mockingbirds, and "musquetoes" were fascinating curiosities of nature. She was enchanted with the exotic plants of the Cape Fear, delighting in the waxy magnolias and huge trumpet honeysuckle. After traveling the Cape Fear River she extolled its beauty:

Nothing can be finer than the banks of this river, a thousand beauties of the flowery and sylvan tribes hang over it.

She was interested in agricultural practice, slavery, social customs, and the role of women. She admired Mrs. Cornelius Harnett and was impressed by her industry. She felt Mary Harnett's long work days presented a sharp contrast to the other "rustic" women, whose approach to work appeared "indolent," but she was bewildered that a lady of position such as Mary Harnett would personally sell her garden produce, eggs, chickens, and homemade pies on Wilmington's streets. She did, however, grudgingly admit that she had met "some most amiable and agreeable acquaintances . . . many of whom would make . . . . art of the world."

As to the town of Wilmington she complained of the unpaved streets that soiled her slippers but observed:

> The people of the town live decently, and 'tho their houses are not spacious, they are in general very commodious and well furnished. All the Merchants of any note are British and Irish, and many of them are very genteel people.

Miss Schaw found the average man's gentility in short supply and characterized many as brutes or beasts. No doubt the frontier bred men of a rougher surface than the more polished gentlemen of Edinburgh and London, although her judgment was colored by a disgust for their politics. Although many of the merchant class were Loyalists, the majority of the people of the Lower Cape Fear found fault with the Crown's colonial policy. Miss Schaw was appalled to report that even Wilmington's ladies " . . . burnt their tea in solemn procession." This was a reference to the Wilmington "tea party" which followed the better-known Boston and Edenton demonstrations. Wilmington ladies had burnt their tea rather than drink it. Miss Schaw was shocked to read the seditious *Cape Fear Mercury,* published by the ardent Whig, Adam Boyd, who had taken over the *Gazette* after its publisher Andrew Steuart had died. She watched the local militia drill and knew that this volunteer force of men between the ages of 16 and 60 formed the backbone of the armed resistance. She scoffed at their scruffy appearance:

> I really must laugh when I recollect their figures: 2000 men in their shirts and trousers, preceded by a very ill-beat drum and a fiddler, who was also in his shirt with a long sword and cue in his hair, who played with all his might. They made indeed a most unmartial appearance.

But she was wise enough to realize that although they lacked the polish of the Redcoats, "the worst figure there can shoot from behind a bush and kill even a General Wolfe."

As Miss Schaw's visit lengthened into the summer of 1775 preparations for war took on a real earnestness. In early September the First Provincial Congress, formed in 1774 in defiance of Governor Martin, ordered two regiments to be raised from North Carolina to serve the Continental Army. Colonel James Moore was appointed to command the First Regiment and then Colonel Robert Howe the Second. Wilmington became one of the province's six military districts.

Governor Martin, knowing his term as colonial governor was finished, dissolved the Provincial Assembly in April 1775. Miss Janet Schaw and other Scottish loyalists were invited aboard the British warship Martin had taken refuge on to escape humiliations such as tar-and-featherings, which were becoming commonplace. In December Miss Schaw boarded another ship and went to Lisbon. She was living back in Edinburgh by 1778.

As the year 1775 came to a close it was estimated that 500 revolutionaries were encamped about Wilmington. Parliament had declared the colonies to be in a state of rebellion. Trade had ceased and the river channel was blockaded with sunken vessels and chains. Josiah Martin devised a strategy which he believed would nip the Whig cause in the bud. He planned a three-pronged attack, using the Loyal Highland Scots of Cross Creek (Fayetteville), the Black Pioneers (free blacks and slaves who had been recruited by the British in exchange for freedom and transportation out of the colony), and British troops from Boston under Sir Henry Clinton. He believed that together they could put down the North Carolina rebellion with ease and then conquer South Carolina, Virginia, and Georgia.

But Martin had not counted on the effective network of patriot intelligence, which kept the American forces—led by Richard Caswell, Alexander Lillington, and James Moore—well informed as to British strategy; nor had he counted on the British squadron under Sir Peter Parker being way behind schedule in arriving at Cape Fear to join forces with Lord Cornwallis' troops. The Loyalist Highlanders had been primed for battle and were eager for action, but at their first skirmish with the patriots at Rockfish Creek, Colonel James Moore successfully repulsed them. Further, the patriots had deduced that the Loyalists would choose the wooden bridge over Widow Moore's Creek as the route to Wilmington for the rendezvous with the British. Acting on this calculation, Lillington ordered the bridge sabotaged; portions of the flooring were removed and the remaining planks and runners were greased with tallow and softsoap to insure treacherous footing. The patriots hid in strategic locations to await their enemy.

The gray dawn of February 27, 1776, barely revealed the rude log bridge silhouetted against the white mists rising from the dark, cold waters below. Thick pine straw served to muffle sounds and the patriots' anxious heavy breathing was indiscernible. Suddenly the skirl of bagpipes pierced the silence. As 1,600 tartan-kilted Highlanders confidently marched toward the bridge, 1,000 concealed patriots opened fire. The Scots tried to take to the woods while those who had fallen into the creek from the slippery bridge tried to scramble ashore, but some drowned or were injured. The battle was short and the casualties were few, but the success of the Battle of Moore's Creek Bridge was a great psychological victory for the patriots. The British had not only been turned back, but they had been humiliated.

The North Carolina sentiment for American independence solidified and then became official in April 1776 when the Fourth Provincial Congress at Halifax resolved that North Carolina would declare its vote for independence, and empowered its delegates to join with the other colonies in declaring independence at the First Continental Congress.

Of the three delegates elected to represent North Carolina at Philadelphia, one was a gentleman of the Lower Cape Fear. His name was William Hooper.

Hooper, like Harnett, had been weaned on ideas and rhetoric, but rather than the informality of a Brunswick tavern, his classroom had the austerity of a wooden pew at Boston's Trinity Church where his father preached each Sunday. Young Hooper's

◆ ◆ ◆

Left: *This 1763 cartoon predicted the flourishing of English commerce with the burial of the Stamp Act. Men of the Cape Fear were proud that their resistance had assisted the defeat of the unfair tax. Courtesy, North Carolina State Archives*
Right: *A large segment of the population in North Carolina was loyal to the Crown. After the Battle of Culloden many Scots emigrated to North Carolina where, true to their oath of allegiance, they remained loyal to the king. Flora MacDonald, a heroine who had aided the Stuart cause, came to Wilmington on behalf of the Loyalists to help raise money for their supplies. Courtesy, North Carolina State Archives*

superior scholarship enabled him to enter Harvard as a sophomore, where he received an M.A., choosing law as his profession. Family friends proposed Hooper set up practice in Wilmington and by 1764 William Hooper was spending many a weary hour in the saddle as he made his rounds throughout North Carolina, following the court circuit. He developed a liking for the Lower Cape Fear but proved susceptible to chronic malaria, which he attributed to the climate.

Hooper married Anne Clark, the daughter of a Wilmington sheriff, in August 1767. The newlyweds set up housekeeping in Wilmington and eventually purchased a parcel of property out of Caleb Grainger's Masonborough Plantation which they named Finian. Hooper hosted many Masonic meetings at Finian where he had an opportunity to fraternize with Cornelius Harnett, Archibald MacLaine, Edward Jones, and Joshua Wright.

By 1769 Hooper was regarded as a talented attorney, a brilliant orator, and a man of character. His progression into politics was inevitable, and his influential colleagues advised him to align himself with the Whig cause. In April 1774, Hooper told James Iredell that he foresaw the colonies "are fast striding to independence and will ere long build an empire upon the ruins of Great Britain." Hooper, along with John Ashe, represented New Hanover County at the First Provincial Congress; and, although he was accused of using unfair campaign tactics, won by a hair the election as a delegate to the First Continental Congress.

At age 32 Hooper returned to his native Northeast as a representative of North Carolina. When he rose to speak even John Adams stopped to listen, noting in his private journal: "Lee [Richard Henry], Henry [Patrick], and Hooper [William] are the orators." While he expressed the desire to retain loyalty to King George III, he

finally came to the conclusion expressed in his sentence:

> That the colonies may continue connected as they have been is our second wish: Our first is that America may be free.

Hooper, like Harnett, was candid about the tedium of serving in Congress. He was disillusioned by the shambles that was the Continental Army and the haggling of congressional committees. When he suffered the humiliation of being re-elected to office by a narrow margin he decided it was time to quit.

In 1777 Hooper returned to Finian. It did not take long for his practice to again flourish and he found himself elected to the general assembly. His personal fortunes seemed to be improving when the word came that the British were approaching Wilmington. Hooper knew that as a signer of the Declaration of Independence he would be a prize captive but, feeling sure that his family would be safe within Wilmington, he went to Hillsborough.

The British returned late in January 1781. News of their approach preceded them and residents were fearful the British would attempt to settle old scores. The man in charge was Major James Henry Craig, a 33-year-old officer who had worn the British uniform since age 15. He had earned the reputation of being "hot, peremptory, and pompous." Craig had been ordered to take Wilmington, establish himself as the conquering commandant, and to secure the Cape Fear River as a supply route into the interior.

He found Wilmington defenseless. As Loyalists came forth to greet their liberator, Whigs fled, went underground, or submissively signed the loyalty oath. Craig commandeered John Burgwin's splendid townhouse because he found it "the most considerable house in town." Part of Craig's strategy in suppressing the patriots was to humiliate them by confiscating their property. He impounded the Hoopers' furniture "in a general sweep" and expelled the family from town. Pews were ripped out of St. James church and horses were stabled there. An old dungeon beneath the Burgwin house was discovered and put to use. A stockade was erected on Market Street in the depression between Second and Third and rumors related the horrible goings-on in the stockade, now known as "Craig's Bull-Pen," and in the dungeon and tunnels under the Burgwin house. David Fanning became Craig's agent to track down, bring in, and torture citizens who were ardent Whigs. Fanning seemed to take perverse pleasure in his work and boasted that women and children were not excluded from his cruelties. Tales of torture circulated; thumbscrews were one of the favored devices. Craig did not limit his activities to Wilmington but sent his emissaries out into the countryside. Plantations were raided and at the Rouse House at least six Americans were bayoneted to death. Craig also ordered the destruction of the Great Bridge that crossed the Northeast River (present location U.S. 117 at the New Hanover-Pender county line). This important drawbridge had been built by Benjamin Heron in 1768 and had the distinction of being the colony's, and perhaps the nation's, first drawbridge.

Even before the British came, there had been concerns among whites that blacks would go over to the British side. Corn-

Far left: *The First Regiment of the North Carolina Continental Army, to which these soldiers belonged, was commanded by Colonel James Moore. Courtesy, North Carolina State Archives*

Left: *Major General Robert Howe commanded the second regiment raised from North Carolina to serve in the Continental Army. A member of Washington's inner circle, he was the only officer south of Virginia to obtain a rank of major general in the Continental Army. Courtesy, Lower Cape Fear Historical Society*

Right: *William Hooper named his summer home overlooking Masonboro Sound "Finian." Here his family could enjoy the prevailing southeastern breezes. Here, too, Hooper hosted Masonic meetings where he had an opportunity to get to know other patriots like Cornelius Harnett, Archibald MacLaine, Edward Jones, and Joshua Wright. Courtesy, Mrs. Ben S. Willis*

wallis and Clinton had actively recruited slaves in 1776 and some 54 local blacks joined the Black Pioneers. Most of the Black Pioneers found themselves delegated to hard labor in the military, with floggings as the disciplinary measure. Some few blacks were given more privileges because they provided good intelligence of the Lower Cape Fear's geography. Black pilots also were invaluable in helping the British travel the booby-trapped channels of the river. The British made extravagant claims as to what rewards they could offer the black volunteers, but the reality was that one kind of bondage was traded for another. Craig enlisted the services of some black coopers and sawyers, but not all slaves were anxious to do the British major's bidding. Mrs. William Hooper's house slave, John, rejected British bribes and escaped Wilmington to travel 70 miles by foot until he overtook his mistress in her flight to join her husband at Hillsborough. Some slaves had chosen to become part of the revolutionary cause by enlisting in the Continental Line or state militia; Primus and Zachariah Jacobs of New Hanover County were two such blacks.

While Craig's despotic reign of terror went on in Wilmington, Lord Cornwallis was about to engage in battle at the courthouse in Guilford County. Cornwallis would later say of the confrontation, "I never saw such fighting since God made me. The Americans fought like demons." Although the British technically won the battle, they suffered a loss of experienced officers and a damaged morale.

Cornwallis determined to march his soldiers to Wilmington. The most ardent Tory could not have taken pride in the pathetic parade of Dragoons who dragged across the coastal plain en route from the Guilford Courthouse to Wilmington. The American campaign had taken its toll. Scarlet tunics had become soiled, dingy, and frayed. If buttons remained they no longer glittered in the sun but were tarnished and dull. Behind the troops came the camp followers. William Dickson of Duplin County wrote:

> They were generally mounted on the best horses dressed in the finest and best clothes that could be taken from the inhabitants as they marched through the country.

Cornwallis arrived in Wilmington in April of 1781 at the head of a demoralized army. Some said that the general seemed bewildered and it was reported that he asked a fellow officer, "What is our plan?" He determined that he would forget the Carolinas and turn his efforts toward Virginia. On April 24, 1781, Cornwallis left Wilmington to march to Yorktown. Tories were invited to leave under his protection and many left Wilmington. Major Craig stayed behind to keep the town in a state of siege. In November the dashing cavalry officer, Colonel Henry (Lighthorse Harry) Lee, brought word that Cornwallis had been defeated at Yorktown and had surrendered to Washington. Craig sailed away from Wilmington, leaving the townspeople to be further subjected to the unscrupulous actions of both Tories and Whigs who wanted to take advantage of the political upheaval.

With the war for independence successfully concluded soldiers began to return home to rebuild the new nation they had fought to create. The Lower Cape Fear welcomed home many a

Top left: *Charles, Lord Cornwallis, arrived in the Wilmington area after a dubious victory at Guilford Courthouse. In an effort to forget the Carolinas, he turned his attention to Virginia. He left on April 25, 1781, to march to Yorktown where Washington's army, supported by the vessels of the French navy, forced his surrender. Courtesy, North Carolina State Archives*

Top right: *Adam Boyd was one of those extraordinary men who represented the 18th-century ideal of the "complete man." He was editor of the* Cape Fear Mercury *and faithfully published provincial news; when war was declared, he joined the Continental Army and became a chaplain; and in 1788 he was ordained a minister of the Episcopal Church and officiated for a short time at St. James Church in Wilmington. Courtesy, Lower Cape Fear Historical Society*

Bottom: *The first lighthouse in North Carolina was erected on Bald Head or Smith's Island at the mouth of the Cape Fear River to warn ships of the treacherous Frying Pan Shoals. Benjamin Smith donated 10 acres of high land on a promontory on Smith's Island overlooking both the river and the sea. From a private collection*

returning soldier, including the Southern colonies' highest ranking officer, Major General Robert Howe. He returned home to find that his ancestral plantation, Kendall, was in a shambles and he set to work to restore his estate.

Howe's ancestors had been involved in the County Clarendon settlement and he was proud of his Lower Cape Fear heritage. He had enjoyed the friendship of Cornelius Harnett and William Hooper and had shared with them the brotherhood of the Masons. He was part of Washington's inner circle, and in 1776 was promoted to the rank of brigadier-general by the Second Continental Congress. He later became commander of the Southern Department, and attained the rank of major-general. But Howe's personal life raised eyebrows and provoked duels. He was legally separated from his wife, and his roving eye caused him no end of trouble with the gentlemen he cuckolded. He was relieved of command of the Southern Department after the loss of the Battle of Savannah in December of 1778, not because of military incompetence, but because his "private amours" had so riled the gentlemen of South Carolina and Georgia. He retained General Washington's blessing, however, and was transferred to the North where he became commander of West Point. He presided over Benedict Arnold's court martial, and was active in forming the North Carolina chapter of the Society of the Cincinnati. Howe retired from military service in 1783 and returned home to Brunswick County where he remained politically active until his death in 1786.

While politicians debated the philosophy that would implement the nation's destiny, Wilmington tried to recover economically. The courts and municipal government made an easy transition from Crown authority to state and local government. Sunken ships impeded the Cape Fear River's navigation, but this was soon remedied and commerce bounced back with the wharves once again lined with naval stores. By 1789 more ships entered the Port of Wilmington than had ever before. The first federal census of 1790 counted 6,800 inhabitants, including 1,000 within Wilmington's town boundaries.

Improved commerce and renewed prosperity in a time of peace fostered entertainments, parties, and festive activities. Around 1788 the Thalians were formed. It is believed that this amateur theatrical group—which took its name from Thalia, the muse of comedy and pastoral poetry—was the first such organization in America. However, the great event that thrilled Wilmington took place in 1791 when President George Washington came to town.

On the outskirts of town at the Rouse House, Captain Henry Toomer and Wilmington's Light Horse Dragoons met the President to escort him to the edge of Wilmington where he was met by the official party. Trumpeting Light Horse Dragoons preceded the President, his entourage, and the dignitaries of Wilmington. The President first went to Dorsey's Tavern where he hosted a dinner for his Wilmington hosts. While at dinner the President remarked that the many swamps he had observed caused him to wonder about the quality of the local drinking water. The tavernkeeper, Lawrence A. Dorsey, is said to have replied that he couldn't comment upon the caliber of local water since he never drank it.

Throughout his visit Washington was a model of cordiality and thoughtfulness. He complimented the abilities and service of local men he had known such as James Innes, Robert Howe, Cornelius Harnett, William Hooper, and Benjamin Smith. He praised

the elegant dinner he enjoyed at Jocelin Tavern, and complimented the lovely ladies who ornamented the Grand Ball given at the assembly hall built in 1776. The *Maria's* deck, spars, and rigging had been festooned with lights; and he displayed delight in the evening's illuminations and bonfires.

Despite his gracious manner, the nation's president was not enchanted by the Lower Cape Fear. He confided to his diary:

> The whole road from Newbern to Wilmington passes through the most barren country I have ever beheld; especially in the parts nearest the latter; which is no more than a bed of white sand.

Washington's tour was made to assure the nation that a stable national government was at work and in good hands. In 1795, when a native son of the Old Cape Fear, Samuel Ashe, was elected North Carolina's governor, the local citizens were further convinced that their state was in good hands. Ashe was linked to one of the region's oldest and most respected families; which had played a major role in the area's development.

As the state government worked to build new institutions, Cape Fear residents worked to rebuild their economy. The University of North Carolina's first student, Hinton James, put his education to work and brought his expertise home by serving as a civil engineer who worked to improve Cape Fear River navigation. Navigation was further improved when the Bald Head Light was completed to warn mariners of the treacherous Frying Pan Shoals. Robert Howe, commissioner of pilotage, and Benjamin Smith, owner of Bald Head, had worked in tandem to accomplish this improvement.

By the end of the century, the town of Wilmington had become more diversified in its religious life. St. James had long been the only congregation with a building and a rector, but Quakers, Baptists, Methodists, and Presbyterians had all had representatives visit and preach in the area. In 1797 an itinerant Methodist preacher named William Meredith arrived with a ministry that was directed to many of the poor of the town. Among his followers were blacks and slaves. Services were held on the outskirts of town and some townspeople resented the bi-racial nature of the services. Someone set fire to the church, but it was too late to halt the enthusiasm of its members, and this humble parish marked the beginning of Methodism in Wilmington.

The year 1798 was marked by a disastrous fire, which found the whole town of Wilmington ablaze. But fire had been a frequent visitor to Wilmington throughout the 18th century, and its citizens had learned to rebuild and go on. As the 18th century drew to a close, the exports of the Cape Fear once again sailed with the high tide and the imports filled the stores to delight eager shoppers anxious to see the latest novelty from abroad. Sailors swaggered into dockside ordinaries and farmers sold their produce under the markethouse. The Port of Wilmington was smug in its success. And it had provided leadership to help build a new nation. On December 31, 1799, the town watchman made his usual midnight rounds. As his familiar, reassuring call broke the night stillness he seemed a soothsayer portending a bright new century for a prosperous young city in the new nation—"Twelve O'Clock and All is Well!"

Through much of the antebellum era, the Port City of Wilmington led North Carolina's parade as the state's biggest, most important town. A new railroad and the great steamers assured Wilmington's ascendancy as a transportation center, and at times her commerce—based on naval stores, the peanut, rice and cotton—surpassed that of Norfolk, Richmond, and Petersburg. Although much of the state suffered serious population loss and enough cultural and commercial stagnation to be dubbed "the Rip Van Winkle state," Wilmington's fortunes continued to wax.

The town was long accustomed to her citizens obtaining important positions and they continued to do so throughout the formation of the new republic. Men of the Lower Cape Fear had worked actively to make independence possible and now the time had come to make it work. Alfred Moore served as justice of the United States Supreme Court. Archibald Maclaine helped frame the state constitution; William Henry Hill served as North Carolina's first United States district attorney. John D. Jones was elected Speaker of the North Carolina House, while Owen Holmes, Griffith John McRee, and Robert Strange French became judges. Law dynasties were established by the Meares and the Wrights; a medical dynasty was established by the deRossets.

Joshua Grainger Wright (1768-1811) qualified to practice law in 1790. He was said to be something of an orator, so he may have put his persuasive powers to work when he convinced the girl who lived next door to his parents' Sound property at Wrightsville to marry him the following year. Susan Bradley Wright's first child was a son, followed by three more, and by 1799 Wright moved his growing family to larger quarters, purchasing John Burgwin's handsome townhouse at Third and Market for "3,500 Spanish milled dollars." The Wrights lived at this address for 50 years. Over the years Wright served as a member of the North Carolina House of Commons, then as speaker of the house, and finally as judge of the Superior Court. His sons Joshua, Charles, and William all followed his profession, while Thomas Henry devoted his energies to finance, becoming president of the region's first bank, the Bank of Cape Fear, chartered in 1804.

It was not surprising that the widower John Burgwin entrusted his first-born daughter, Eliza, to the Wrights' care when she returned to America from England in 1801. Eliza had enjoyed life abroad; she had acquired a fine education and a taste for bright society. Her manners made her agreeable, but to her diary she confided that she found Wilmington's social set somewhat provincial. One night she went with her chaperones, the Wrights, to a party. The chic young woman represented the latest in English style:

> My dress was a sprigg'd India muslin with a drapery trimm'd with lace and an ostrich feather, fasten'd with a silver bandeau. My hair curl'd short all over my head . . . a gold chain, and no other adornment . . .

She got to the party to find not an orchestra, but only the disagreeable "scrape" of a single violin; she found the style of dancing "quite strange" and the local ladies' dress "more so . . ."

> powder'd curls, down the back—Morocco shoes and cotton stockings—color'd underdresses and stiff plain and figur'd muslin over.

Despite Eliza's reservations about Wilmington's fashion quotient, she met a young doctor that evening named George Clitherall who interested her more than the local customs. Twenty-five years later, as Eliza Burgwin Clitherall, her diary would take on a more somber note as she reflected on the last days of the tempestuous Cape Fear aristocrat the North Carolina General Assembly had chosen as governor in 1810.

Benjamin Smith (1756-1826) needed no middle name to set him apart from other Smiths. He commanded and demanded attention. His detractors found him vain, arrogant, self-seeking, opinionated, and vindictive. His admirers thought him generous, talented, hospitable, gracious, progressive, and patriotic. He was all of these and more; his multifaceted personality precipitated both his triumphs and his ruin.

He wore his distinguished ancestry like a bright royal blue boutonniere that set him above men of lesser lineage. His illustrious forebears included Thomas Smith (the first landgrave), Sir John Yeamans, and "King" Roger Moore. He married Sarah Rhett Dry, daughter of the Brunswick port collector. Her blood and fortunes matched his own, and although she bore no children and suffered humiliations because of her husband's ugly temper and financial losses, her cheerful disposition, love, and loyalty never failed him.

Together the Smiths dispensed a lavish hospitality. Sarah's garden was renowned for its flowers and produce. Their table was well-appointed and groaned under the weight of choice delicacies and vintages. They entertained at Blue Banks (a 3,800-acre plantation in Brunswick County), at Belvedere, at a townhouse in Wilmington, a summerhouse in Smithville, and at their pleasure house, Sea Castle, on Bald Head Island. But their principal place of residence was Orton Plantation, which the Smiths had bought but eventually were forced to sell. In 1790, 221 slaves—the largest number owned by one man in North Carolina—tilled their fields, ran the sawmills, and served their needs. Brunswick County became Smith's private fiefdom and his subjects were deftly manipulated to do his bidding.

Smith became head of the Wilmington District of Militia, which led to his rank of general, a title he bore with pride until it was replaced by governor. He finagled the incorporation of the town of Smithville (modern-day Southport) and had it named for himself. His egotism created enemies, but he also displayed a magnanimity that was grandiose. His Revolutionary War service merited a gift of

Governor Edward Bishop Dudley was a man of high principles. He served in the Twenty-first Congress but declined an invitation to run for reelection saying, "Congress is not a place for an honest man." He was a leader in the movement to bring a railroad to Wilmington. Courtesy, North Carolina State Archives

Chartered in 1804, the Bank of Cape Fear had an authorized capital of $250,000. It was the larger of two banks in the state. Later it became the First National Bank of Wilmington. From the North Carolina Collection, UNC Library, Chapel Hill

Wilmington had its share of professional dynasties and the law was no exception. William Belvedere Meares (shown here) read law with Judge William Gaston at Chapel Hill early in the 19th century. His sons, Oliver, Thomas, and Gaston, as well as two grandsons, became attorneys. Courtesy, Henry Jay MacMillan

William Henry Hill of the illustrious Hill family studied law in Boston, taught school in the Cape Fear area, and was a merchant at Brunswick. He was appointed the first United States District Attorney for the District of North Carolina and later served in the North Carolina Senate and in the United States Congress. Courtesy, Lower Cape Fear Historical Society

This engraving of Third and Market streets appeared in Ballou's magazine in the 1850s. St. James Church and the Burgwin-Wright house still dominate the intersection. Courtesy, Lower Cape Fear Historical Society

Caroline Eliza Burgwin Clitherall, reared by her grandparents in England, returned to Wilmington when she was 17 or 18 years old to live at the Hermitage with her father John Burgwin. While still a girl, Eliza began a diary that she kept intermittently throughout her life. Her observations of people and social conditions give us fresh insight into life at the turn of the 19th century. Courtesy, Mrs. Gray Zouck

Benjamin Smith, a Revolutionary War officer and a governor of North Carolina, was an imposing figure in the Cape Fear area as well as the whole of North Carolina. While his detractors found him vain, arrogant, self-seeking, opinionated, and vindictive, his admirers thought him generous, talented, hospitable, gracious, progressive, and patriotic. He was all of these and more; his multi-faceted and complex personality both enabled his triumphs and precipitated his ruin. Courtesy, North Carolina State Archives

20,000 acres in Tennessee, which he transferred to the University of North Carolina, resulting in his appointment to the Board of Trustees. He acted as surety for Colonel Reed, Wilmington's port collector. He also espoused progressive ideas, used his political influence to push support for public and higher education, advocated scientific agricultural practice, proposed modern penal codes, including a penitentiary system, and worked for improved navigation and commerce. As governor he had made many progressive proposals to the Legislature (most were rejected), and as a public man he continued to advocate his ideas through letters, speeches, and influence throughout his lifetime.

As he aged, his temper grew worse, and he indulged in personal slander and abuse that resulted in more than one duel. He recovered from the duels, but increasing financial difficulties were not so easily mended. Port Collector Reed had defaulted on his loan, which saddled Smith with enormous debt. His difficulties were compounded by speculation, and gradually he began to lose everything, including his health. His friends drifted away; but his physician, Dr. George Clitherall, and his wife, Smithville's school mistress, the former Eliza Burgwin, remained loyal to the failing Smith. They had attended Sarah Smith on the night she died, as a storm raged around her.

On yet another stormy night in 1826, the Clitheralls found the former governor at Smithville, on his deathbed. Eliza recalled Smith's last night when he asked: "Where is the text which says, 'Set thy house in order for surely thou must die'?" Eliza wrote:

> . . . with every gust of wind, slam after slam; the waves so near the dwelling, sent their spray with every rolling billow against the glass, the large door blew open, nor could the strength of one man close it. . . . The impressions of that awful night, can never be effaced. The spirit of speculation had entirely impoverished this once wealthy owner of vast territory . . . his last and third plantation had been seized and sold. Sales at auction, and by law, had scattered his hundreds of slaves . . .

Smith's burial was secret so that his creditors could not claim his corpse. Few mourned him, and of the former governor the February 17, 1826 *Raleigh Register* only printed, "General Benjamin Smith died recently in Brunswick County."

An obituary in the *Wilmington Gazette* of May 12, 1812 had run longer:

> Died on the 11th instant, William Campbell, Esq., a native of this town, at the advanced age of 78 years, being the first white child born in this place.

Campbell did not live until June 18 when the formal declaration of war against Great Britain came. Almost immediately, North Carolina began to mobilize and Captain Jacob Hartman organized the Wilmington Volunteer Artillery, North Carolina's only fully-equipped artillery company. South Carolina's Thomas Pinckney was

made Major General of the Sixth District which included the Carolinas, Georgia, and Virginia; he had the formidable task of putting together an army. As recruits enlisted they joined local militias at established fortifications. Fort Johnston had a new battery and began to bulge with equipment and men. But the Fort Johnston recruiters had their problems, for the fort was described by one soldier as "an obscure garrison" infested with "powerful sand flies and bloodthirsty mosquitos." Another wrote home that all he could say for it was that the local people "had warm hearts and there was an early spring."

The navy also had to be mobilized and Wilmington was placed under the protection of Sailing Master Thomas N. Gautier. He feared that Bald Head would become a rendezvous for enemy ships and begged for a bigger fleet to patrol it, although opinions differed as to how much of a threat there was to Wilmington. Port Collector Robert Cochran advised preparedness but doubted if real danger was imminent.

A full-scale invasion never did occur, but what made the War of 1812 most real to the people of Wilmington was privateering. More than 526 American ships carried official letters of marque and their captured prizes were a frequent harbor sight. In 1814, 15 captured British ships were brought into Wilmington, and lively legal battles ensued as to the disposition of the booty. Wilmington even had her own privateering vessel, *The Lovely Lass*, but her career was short. Instead it was the career of a handsome young naval officer named Johnston Blakely who captured Wilmington's heart as its own

1812 war hero.

In 1783 John and Mary Blakely and their two-year-old son, Johnston, left their home in County Down, Ireland to emigrate to the Carolinas, taking up permanent residence in Wilmington. After Mary Blakely and an infant son contracted fever and died, John found companionship among the Masons, where a fellow Irishman, Ed Jones, convinced him that young Johnston would benefit from life in the Jones household. There he was remembered as a young man "who was cheerful and happy when at home" and who had jet black hair, a winning smile, and sparkling bright eyes.

While Johnston was at the University of North Carolina, his father died. He had left his son considerable rental property in Wilmington, but when the property was destroyed in the fire of 1798, Johnston was left with no income. He was forced to leave the university, and although Ed Jones offered to help, Johnston only wished Jones to help him get into the navy. With Jones' help, he obtained an appointment as a midshipman, taking to life on the sea like the proverbial duck to water, and by 1813 he was assigned to command the sloop of war, the *Wasp*. During the year of the *Wasp*'s fitting-out, Johnston had enough leave ashore to court and marry Jane Ann Hooper. Shortly after he wed, he took the *Wasp* to sea with her crew of 173. One of them wrote:

The *Wasp* was a beautiful ship and the finest sea-boat, I believe, in the world . . . Captain Blakely is a brave and discrete officer—as cool and collected in action as at the table . . .

The Bank of Cape Fear issued this five-dollar bill. Courtesy, North Carolina State Archives

Top: *A flatboat was used from earliest times as a ferry between Wilmington and Eagles' Island, carrying both passengers and freight, and often bringing large groups of horses, cows, and pigs to market. Courtesy, North Carolina State Archives*

Middle: *The* Prometheus *made her maiden voyage on the Cape Fear River in 1817. She was the first steam-driven paddlewheeler on the river and her regular runs between Fayetteville, Wilmington, and Smithville improved commerce. Captain Thomas N. Gautier, a veteran of the War of 1812, ran the steamship for many years. Courtesy, North Carolina State Archives*

Bottom: *This scene of Wilmington's waterfront was drawn in 1837 from the vantage point of a ship anchored in the Cape Fear River. It is thought to be the wharf of Richard Bradley, a Wilmington merchant. Courtesy, New Hanover County Museum*

The *Wasp* captured the nation's attention when she took the *Reindeer,* a British warship of 21 guns, and in one month destroyed 13 British merchant ships. Congress voted to give Blakely a gold medal plus a formal resolution of thanks, and the North Carolina legislature decided to give her native son a ceremonial silver sword upon his triumphant return home. But there was no return home and while people waited for word, they only learned that Mrs. Blakely had given birth to a daughter, Udney Maria. A wave of public sentiment resulted in the legislature taking the unprecedented action of voting to finance Udney Maria's education, paying $600 per year until 1819. Johnston Blakeley's widow remarried a few years later, and moved to Saint Croix, where Udney Maria also married, but died soon afterward in childbirth.

Saint Croix was also home to a family of struggling Sephardic Jews, Phillip and Rebecca de Mendes Benjamin. Rebecca's uncle, Jacob Levy, wrote from Wilmington that he had become a successful merchant; he said that Jews could earn a living in Wilmington, and he urged the Benjamins to emigrate to North Carolina where he would help them become established. They arrived in 1813, and the family soon became absorbed into the Levy household. As a toddler, their son, Judah, scampered around the coffers piled with "Turks Island salt, prime green coffee, West Indian and New England rum, sugar, crockery, glassware, padlocks, Negro cloths, callicoes, and assorted articles" sold at Levy and Gomez's Auction Sales. The Levy and Benjamin families later moved to Fayetteville, but half a century later some Wilmingtonians could still recall young Judah Benjamin, who grew up to become attorney general, secretary of war, and secretary of state of the Confederacy.

The Benjamins might have ridden to Fayetteville on the newfangled river sensation — the steamboat. In 1817 the first steam-driven paddlewheeler, *The Prometheus,* made her Cape Fear River debut, with War of 1812 naval veteran Thomas N. Gautier at the helm. As the steamer approached the Dram Tree, bells were rung and cannons were fired to announce her approach. Crowds swarmed the wharves and were not disappointed in the dramatic show that ensued. The paddlewheeler had to fight a fierce current and ebbing tide that demanded every engine's valiant effort. Captain Gautier cracked orders through his brass horn to the engineer below, "Give it to her, Snyder!" Snyder did, and the reverberating engines screamed in reply to delight the crowd. The steam monster proved her mettle and soon was joined by another paddlewheeler, the *Henrietta.* One dollar bought a one-way fare to Smithville, and with luck the trip took about four hours.

Two years later Wilmington's rising prosperity was to be painfully interrupted by two old enemies. The yellow fever epidemic spread through the town almost as voraciously as the devastating fire that followed it, burning down more than 300 buildings. The situation in 1819 was so desperate that the citizens of Raleigh, as well as both houses of the state legislature, helped raise funds to rebuild Wilmington; the Presbyterians raised $6,000 to rebuild their church. The Cape Fear River was the constant in the community that helped the town revive. It was necessary to keep the channel open and the federal government took over improvements in 1829, ensuring Wilmington's development as a major port.

The unique river port provided a nautical heritage of which Cape Fear historian, James Sprunt, eloquently wrote. He remembered "the anchor lights of half a hundred ships twinkling off their moorings," of sailors singing "Larboard, Watch Ahoy," and of the sea chanties heard on every wharf. Eliza Burgwin Clitherall recalled the gifts from the ships: ". . . a basket of oranges and pineapples, a sack of coffee, a jar of Tamarinds." Local newspapers printed the lyrics of such songs as "The Song of the Sea Shell," "The Return of the Oyster; A Hard Shell Lyric," and "Two Real Tars, Whom Duty Called." But underneath the salty sophistication of the Port City lay serious problems. Sailors carried disease, became drunk, caused disruptions; and they were often lonely or destitute. A port quarantine officer coped with disease, but a group of gentlemen confronted the other difficulties by establishing the Seaman's Friend Society — its aims were "to improve the social, moral, and religious conditions of the seamen," as well as to provide them with a boarding house and hospital.

The port provided a strong commerce that supported improvements and by the mid-1850s Wilmington could boast three shipyards, some fine plank roads, and a railroad. But Wilmington still had its rustic side, one citizen complaining to the *Advertiser* about hogs running loose in the streets. Mortimer DeMott, a visitor from New York, also criticized the town's provincialism, but was intrigued by the racial makeup of the community in which he assessed "one half of the population of this place to be black." His guess was accurate. In 1830 New Hanover County had 4,921 whites, 5,497 slaves, and 341 free blacks.

In 1829 David Walker, a Wilmington black born to a slave father and a free mother, published in Boston *An Appeal in Four Articles Together With a Preamble to the Colored Citizens of the World,* urging slaves to throw off their bondage and overthrow their masters. Abolitionists and the slave underground circulated the *Appeal,* which surfaced in Wilmington in about 1830. Its rhetoric terrified the local authorities and near hysteria ensued when the news of the Nat Turner revolt in Virginia became known the next year. Shortly thereafter the Sampson County sheriff learned that plans for a slave uprising were already in motion, and would culminate at Wilmington where 2,000 armed slaves would gather. Approaches to Wilmington were heavily guarded and United States troops from Fort Monroe augmented the local militia. The suspected ringleaders were rounded up and sentences included public whippings and hangings at Gallows Hill near Ninth and Princess. Those who were executed were decapitated and their heads were placed on pikes in conspicuous places to serve as a warning. Abolitionists intensified their efforts, and local tradition states that the many tunnels along the Wilmington waterfront were used to transport runaways. Buddy Wright, a Wilmington fugitive who successfully reached Boston reported: ". . . boats were stationed in the mouth of the Cape Fear . . . to take fugitives North." The threatened insurrection brought tightened restrictions on the movements of slaves, but practicality won out and by 1835 whites were petitioning that slaves be allowed to work on the docks.

The bustling docks had contributed to Wilmington's success. In 1830 the Richmond Compiler admitted: "We have been surprised to hear that the tonnage of Wilmington exceeds that of Richmond, although the town had not one fourth our population." In that same year, a Northerner, "P.K." Dickinson, initiated a new link in the town's transportation network. Dickinson had moved to Wilmington where he invested his considerable energy and capital into lumber. After seeing a railroad operating in New England he felt sure that this was what Wilmington needed, and convinced his influential friends of the same. By 1833 a concerted effort advocating a railroad from Wilmington to Raleigh was being mounted at the state level.

In 1835 a group of Wilmington's most prominent citizens gathered before the fire in the Yellow Room of future governor Edward Bishop Dudley's house to discuss financing the railroad. The host led the proceedings with a personal pledge of $25,000, and when the meeting was over the men in the room had subscribed an amount that exceeded Wilmington's entire tax evaluation.

Construction of the railroad began the next year. Raleigh had hedged on its obligations so the rails were rerouted toward Weldon. Construction brought some unwelcome intruders in the form of exotic weeds from Europe and the West Indies—they accompanied the ballast stones imported to support the railroad, and have thrived ever since. On March 7, 1840, the last spike was driven in the 161-1/2-mile track, which at that time was the world's longest span. A noisy celebration of this feat took place on April 5. Every flag that could be found flew, cannons fired on the quarter-hour, bands played, crowds gathered, paraders marched, and the day ended with a festive banquet celebrating the completion of the Wilmington and Weldon Railroad.

The new Wilmington and Weldon Railroad building went up in flames in 1843 when the town was once again afflicted by fire. Again its citizens dug deep into their pockets, borrowed, and started over. The man who had launched the railroad subscription drive also pledged his personal fortune to underwrite rebuilding costs after the 1843 fire. Governor Edward Bishop Dudley (1789-1855) lived in the handsome brick house at Front and Nun, which commanded a view of the river. Dudley was considered a man of high principle. He served in the Twenty-first Congress but declined a re-election bid saying "Congress is not a place for an honest man."

Governor Dudley was a generous, congenial host who entertained such notables as Henry Clay and Daniel Webster. In 1845 Dudley's daughter, Jane Frances, married a young United States Army officer. The couple exchanged vows in front of the massive marble fireplace in the dining room. The bride was attended by a bevy of cousins and friends, while the groom surrounded himself with fellow officers resplendent in blue uniforms. One of the groomsmen, a young lieutenant, was so delighted with the three-day round of parties and balls that when he returned to North Carolina 20 years later as the conquering General William T. Sherman, he remarked, upon meeting Wilmingtonian Colonel John D. Taylor, that he still remembered the Dudley wedding.

As the town struggled to rebuild itself, once again it returned to the river for sustenance, nurturing it by subscribing $60,000 to deepen the channel. The harbor master reported more arrivals in port with every passing year—667 in 1847. But a hefty percentage of the area's commerce still depended on the forest. Edward Kidder, of Potter and Kidder's sawmill enterprise, discovered how to turn sawdust into fuel, which brought higher profits for the mill operators. In 1844 P.K. Dickinson, who had helped bring the railroad to Wilmington, began building a new steam sawmill to join those of the

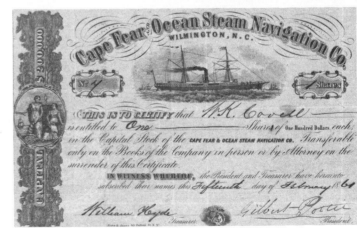

Facing page, top: *Judah Phillip Benjamin and his parents emigrated in 1813 to Wilmington from Saint Croix. Although the family later moved to Fayetteville, Wilmingtonians were proud of the boy who grew up to become a United States Senator, Confederate States Attorney General, Secretary of War, and Jefferson Davis' Secretary of State. Courtesy, The Historic New Orleans Collection*

Bottom: *The growing commerce of the port of Wilmington provided many opportunities for businessmen to engage in profit-making ventures. Courtesy, Lower Cape Fear Historical Society*

This page, top: *In a typical turpentine camp in the Lower Cape Fear raw materials were loaded on a tramway and taken to a distillery near Wilmington. Courtesy, North Carolina State Archives*

Middle: *In distilleries near Wilmington the rosin from the pine tree was processed into turpentine. Courtesy, North Carolina State Archives*

Bottom: *The dense forests of the Cape Fear provided raw material for sawmills such as this one on Point Peter, opposite Wilmington. With the advent of steam, two gangs of saws could cut 140,000 feet of timber daily, which meant 105,000 feet of lumber. From the North Carolina Collection, UNC Library, Chapel Hill*

A TURPENTINE DISTILLERY, WILMINGTON, N. C.

town's many established firms. Two gangs of saws cut 140,000 feet of timber daily, turning out 105,000 board feet of lumber. In addition to the sawmills, nine turpentine distilleries and 30 stills produced 800 barrels of turpentine and 4,000 gallons of spirits-of-turpentine daily. The 1845 *Chronicle* noted:

> The turpentine distilled in this place last year is estimated at 200,000 barrels, worth $400,000. The raw material shipped 74,000 barrels, valued at $68,000. Tar shipped 30,000 barrels worth $45,000. Total $513,000. A tolerable respectable revenue from one tree. Long live the evergreen pine.

Along with innovations in the lumber industry, the mid-century was marked by a number of successful commercial ventures such as the founding of the Wilmington Gas and Light Company in 1854, which replaced the old whale lamps with gaslight. That same year travelers could make new connections via the Wilmington, Charlotte, and Rutherford Railroad. In 1859 the Wilmington fertilizer business was launched by the incorporation of the Navassa Guano Company of Wilmington, after the discovery of tons of this superior fertilizer on the island of Navassa in the West Indies.

Part of the town's commerce came from the lowly ground pea, or peanut, which was successfully exported from several plantations between Rich and Mason Inlets. For a time, Wilmington was the South's largest exporter of peanuts. Nicholas N. Nixon of Porter's Neck Plantation was the biggest producer in the early antebellum period.

Prosperity enriched Wilmington on many fronts. It brought a new sophistication, more culture, and allowed for philanthropy. Reading rooms were established and were frequented by "intelligent citizens who liked to meet daily to enjoy the pleasures of reading and conversation." A Literary Society was formed, evolving into the Lyceum which maintained a library and sponsored public lectures.

Throughout the antebellum period a number of private schools were organized and enjoyed a brief period of popularity. Miss Laura Rankin ran a successful school, as did Colonel Carter Jones who taught infantry drills, "together with broadsword exercises and cavalry movements." The gentry favored the Jewett's school—run by Stephen and George Jewett—for strict discipline and high academic standards.

The first free school had been provided for by French and Indian war hero James Innes' will prior to the Revolution, but the war interrupted its progress and it was not until 1800 that the Innes Academy opened its doors at Third and Princess Streets. By mid-century, the public school movement was still in its infancy although Dr. Frederick Hill lobbied in Raleigh to build a good system. Wealthy families who did not patronize the town's private schools sent their children away to school or hired tutors. The public school superintendent, S.D. Wallace, reported in 1852: "I am sorry to say that in Wilmington our common schools are not patronized except by those who have not the means to send their children to other schools." The black population had no school at all.

Some education was provided by the churches, along with many charitable projects. The Ladies Working Society of St. James sponsored a free school for whites, and around 1840 six Methodist ladies formed the Ladies' Benevolent Society with Catherine deRosset Kennedy as president. By 1879 the society was sponsoring the Old Ladies Rest, which evolved into the Catherine Kennedy Home—possibly the oldest institution for the aged in the country.

As the city grew it demanded new buildings. Aaron Lazarus' planing mill provided much of the lumber and two builders from Nantucket, Robert Barclay Wood and his brother John C. Wood, arrived in Wilmington to build whatever the town needed. Their first major contract was the erection of the new St. James. Thomas U. Walter of Philadelphia designed the building, but New York architect, John S. Norris, who had established a fine reputation in Savannah, supervised the Wood brothers' construction. While St. James was being built another fire swept Wilmington. The Bank of Cape Fear sustained enough damage to warrant remodeling and a new customs house was also needed; Norris picked up both of these architectural assignments. The Wood brothers went on to construct almost every significant public building and house during the antebellum period.

Wilmington experienced a new cultural diversity in the antebellum years, as a growing population spawned new churches, enterprises, and entertainments. As early as 1800, more than 200 citizens participated in a St. Andrew's Day celebration, with gay Scottish reels added to the regular dance sets. By 1807 there were enough Irish to observe a St. Patrick's Day party at Laurence Dorsey's tavern. French Huguenots added such lovely names as Madeline and Gabriella to the baptismal records, while slave uprisings in Haiti brought an additional influx of Frenchmen so that French surnames such as Poisson and Formy-Duval became part of Wilmington's directory.

Commercial growth attracted enterprising immigrants such as the 400 to 500 Germans who had come to the Port City by the late 1850s. Many became merchants and their thrift and hard work contributed to the town's growth. The German community organized a military company, and initiated the founding of the St. Paul Lutheran Church in 1859. St. Paul's Episcopal Church had been formed the year before, and the Presbyterians had built their second church on Chestnut and MacRae. The Baptists, who had established a small congregation in 1808, launched a drive to build the First Baptist Church at Fifth and Market by the middle of the century.

It was Judge William Gaston who inspired a new ecumenism on the state level. Prior to 1835, Article 32 of the North Carolina constitution prohibited public office to anyone who was not a Protestant. Out of respect for Gaston, the law was changed to prohibit public office only to those who were not "Christian." But in 1858 the small Jewish community in Wilmington petitioned the legislature to "remove from the fundamental law of the State this last remnant of bigotry and prejudice." After the Civil War, the article was amended to read that a person would be debarred from holding office only if he denied the existence of God.

In 1860, of North Carolina's 157,014 churchgoers, only 350 professed Catholicism. Clearly the Reverend Thomas Murphy had his work cut out for him when he arrived in Wilmington in 1845 to do missionary work; he found 40 Catholics in the town, and no Catholic church. The Wilmington establishment was not anxious to allow a group of practicing Papists in their midst, and a concerted effort had been made not to sell property to a priest. Catherine Ann McKoy, Dr. William A. Berry, and Bernard Baxter pooled their money and purchased property on Dock Street between Second and Third, then gave it to the church. The Gothic revival church featured lancet windows, drawing upon St. James for architectural inspiration. The ceremonial laying of the cornerstone took place in May 1846, as crowds gawked at the ornate vestments of Charleston's visiting clergy. As was the custom of the time, white church members proselytized their black slaves to their own faith, and in 1849 Father Murphy stood at the baptismal font of the church of St. Thomas the Apostle to baptize a slave, Maria Anna Jones, and her four children, as North Carolina's first black Catholics.

By 1847 Wilmington had seven established congregations, and in the years to come a new sect would add a church whose founder had once lived in Wilmington. Mary Baker, a pretty, pensive girl of strict Calvinist background who was often homebound because of ill health, married a brick mason, George Washington Glover, in 1843, who convinced her to move from her native New Hampshire to Charleston, South Carolina. While there, he learned that Wilmington needed brick masons to help rebuild the fire-devastated town, and the couple arrived in Wilmington in 1844, setting up housekeeping at Hanover House. Mary, who soon realized she was pregnant, passed the time by writing verse, while her husband plied his trade. But in June, he began to show signs of the dread yellow fever, and died within nine days, leaving Mary bereft, far from family and home, and low on funds. St. John's Masons rallied around her, paid her bills, and arranged for a burial at St. James. When she left Wilmington, the townspeople remembered Mary Baker Glover only as a young widow who had been touched by the kindness of her friends. But she later became known as one of America's foremost spiritual leaders, when, as Mary Baker Eddy, she founded the Church of Christ, Scientist.

At a time when pneumonia, appendicitis, yellow fever, typhoid, diphtheria, and blood poisoning often were fatal, death became a too-frequent visitor. By 1852 it was apparent that Wilmington needed a cemetery. A committee purchased a 65-acre tract on the east side of Burnt Creek. Dr. Armand deRosset was elected president and Charles Quigley was hired as superintendent of the Oakdale Cemetery. Ironically, the first burial to take place there was for Dr. deRosset's six-year-old daughter, Annie.

Despite the number of bereaved families who mourned at the cemetery's graveside monuments during the antebellum period, the townspeople did enjoy the popular diversions of the era. Horse racing was favored by both blacks and whites. Newspapers published notices of the "Wilmington Turf," and a local favorite, "Touchstone," even inspired a popular song. The amount of alcohol and gambling that accompanied the races partially inspired Wilmington's wives, mothers, and sweethearts to pressure their menfolk into signing the North Carolina Temperance Society's pledge. They succeeded in winning over 400 Wilmingtonians to the side of temperance.

Steamboats provided the transportation for river excursions such as the one to Smithville (Southport) aboard the barrel-shaped steamer, Spray. Romantics loved her moonlight cruises, and popular love songs filled the night air. Crowds went by steamer to Smithville for the glorious Fourth of July festivities, which have evolved into the modern-day North Carolina Fourth of July festival. No holiday was complete without music. May Day was a favorite with young girls, who danced around the May pole in the wooded grove by the Lazarus House on Mulberry (now Grace) Street between Third and Fourth. Minstrel shows were popular entertainment, as were bands.

Wilmington celebrated Christmas in a unique way during the antebellum period because of the custom known as "Kunering." Although little is known about the origins of the custom, it is known that the custom had been introduced by black slaves from West Africa, by way of the West Indies. The tradition was incorporated into Wilmington's Christmas celebrations. It was sometimes called "John Kannaus," "Cannus," or "Kuners." Harriet Brent Jacobs, a slave, recalled the custom:

> Every child rises on Christmas morning to see the John Kannaus. Without them Christmas would be shorn of its greatest attraction . . . a box covered with sheepskin is called the gumbo box. A dozen beat on this while others strike triangles and jawbones to which a band of dancers keep time. For a month previous they are composing songs.

Recollections vary as to the precise lyrics, but almost everyone agrees that one of the songs sung by gaily costumed and masked singers included:

> Ha! Low! Here we go! (repeated thrice)
> Kuners come from Denby.

After the Kuners had grouped together they traveled from house to house to give their performance and to receive a gift.

By the mid-19th century, the local amateur theatrical group, the Thalians, had begun to work with the Town of Wilmington to construct a building that would house a theater and a town hall. After much compromise, John Montague Trimble, a New York architect known for his fine theater buildings, was contracted to draw up the plans. James Francis Post supervised the project, and his meticulous ledger tells the story of the building's long and complex construction. Although the cornerstone was laid in 1855, the elaborate drop curtain, painted by the noted romantic realist, William Thompson Russell Smith, was not installed until 1858. It was described as "a spectacle worth paying the price of admission to see." On opening night, spectators craned their necks to see the white and gilt interior with its beautiful boxes and impressive proscenium arch. Although there was nothing but praise for the grand new addition to Wilmington, there was bitter argument as to who was responsible for the final cost of $17,815.89 ($10,000 over the original estimate). The debate over expenditures received almost as much coverage as the theatrical performances in Wilmington's newspapers.

Since 1851 Wilmington had enjoyed a daily newspaper, The Wilmington Daily Journal, and a number of weekly newspapers, such as The Wilmington Weekly, appeared throughout the antebellum period. Talcott Burr's newspaper, The Herald, was hailed for its journalistic distinction throughout the state. As the issues of slavery, states' rights, and secession heated up, readers were eager to know the political bent of each publisher. As readers took note of where each publisher had been born and where he stood on the issues, arguments and name-calling often ensued. Asa Brown, editor of the Chronicle, had been born in Rhode Island; Edward Cantwell of the Wilmington Light Infantry took exception to one of Brown's editorials and called Brown a Northerner with anti-slavery leanings; Brown countered by calling Cantwell a "South Carolina squatter."

Most Wilmingtonians considered themselves patriotic Americans who loved the Union, but by 1861 the subject of secession was being hotly debated. Local historian James Sprunt wrote:

> In 1861 the great shadow of a great national calamity
> appeared — the whole country was convulsed with conflicting
> emotions . . . the political leaders of North Carolina were divided
> upon the issue . . . It is difficult for those of us who remember only
> the intense unanimity of the Southern people after the War was
> fairly inaugurated to realize how in those previous troubled days the
> minds of men were perplexed with doubts. Up to this time the
> Union sentiment had been in the ascendant.

Sides were being taken; military companies marched incessantly. Secession advocates wore rosettes or badges made of sandburs. Northerners residing in Wilmington had to decide which side to support. Some left town and some cast their lots with their adopted home. The Wilmington Light Infantry's ranks swelled with the town's elite — the company would provide the Confederacy with 57 officers. In January 1861, overzealous Cape Fear Minute Men — a recently organized committee of safety — left Wilmington for Smithville, where they took possession of Fort Johnston, the United States barracks. There they were joined by the Smithville Guards and went on to capture Fort Caswell, but North Carolina Governor John Ellis sent orders to give the forts back to the soldiers in blue, reminding them that North Carolina had not yet seceded from the Union.

Despite the tense political atmosphere, life went on in Wilmington and the town's oldest families — whose complex kinship had been termed by some "the Cousinhood" — still honored the happy occasions of births, baptisms, debuts, and weddings. John Allan Taylor had built a handsome marble house on Market near Fifth Avenue for his bride, Catherine McIlhenny Harriss, in 1847. Twelve years later, just up the street, Dr. John Dillard Bellamy built a great mansion for his wife, Mary Priscilla Jennings Harriss, who was Catherine Harriss Taylor's niece. It was only natural that these neighboring relatives should come together to fete two newlywed couples of their kinship. Dr. Bellamy's daughter, Ellen, recalled the March 1861 party:

> I must tell of a party or "housewarming" my parents gave
> soon after moving in their new home, pronounced the grandest party
> ever held in Wilmington! It was complimentary to two bridal
> couples in our family connection . . . I can remember how beautiful
> everything was, especially the long table set in the dining room with
> everything conceivably good. Hot drink and food brought from the
> kitchen across the hall . . . the end of the back piazza was enclosed
> with blinds and there sat a band which discoursed delightful music
> all during the evening. That was in March — the weddings having
> taken place in February. The War actually broke out April 12th and
> ended all entertaining . . .

Perhaps Ellen Bellamy's fond recollections reflect a partisan pride in her description of "the grandest party ever held in Wilmington," but hindsight served her well to know that the grand-scale entertaining of the antebellum period was at an end. Behind the great Bellamy mansion stood a less imposing brick house, which sheltered the house slaves. They, too, heard the "delightful music" of that spring night. One can only wonder if any of the listeners knew that the Port City parade was about to march to a somber cadence.

◆ ◆ ◆

Facing page, top: *Mary Baker Glover Eddy came to Wilmington as a bride in 1844 and left as a widow a few months later. Thomas Brown, the silversmith and leader of St. John's Masonic Lodge, helped the young woman arrange for her husband's burial in St. James Cemetery, and accompanied the widow back to New England. It is said that after Mrs. Baker founded the new religion of Christian Science that she extended a hand of friendship to the Masons because of her experience with the brotherhood in Wilmington. Courtesy, Lower Cape Fear Historical Society*

Bottom: *The members of the First Baptist Church bought a lot on the corner of Market and Fifth streets in 1858 and immediately began construction of their new sanctuary. Building was interrupted by the Civil War, and the unfinished steeple provided an observation tower to view the advancement of the Federal forces following the fall of Fort Fisher in 1865. Courtesy, Lower Cape Fear Historical Society*

This page, top: *The Masonic Brotherhood was one of the Lower Cape Fear's oldest organizations, and by 1804 they had laid the "anglestone" for their lodge which still stands on Orange Street. The 1819 fire threatened the lodge but the ingenious Masons covered the building with wet blankets and formed a bucket brigade to the river. St. John's has been a Masonic lodge, private home, school, tavern, and is now the administrative headquarters for the St. John's Museum of Art complex. Sketch by Henry Bacon. Courtesy, Miss Elizabeth F. McKoy*

Bottom: *John Montague Trimble, a well known architect of American theaters, designed the City Hall-Thalian Hall complex which held city offices and a theater under one roof. The community has always prided itself on this impressive structure. From a private collection.*

St. John's Lodge
Wilmington, N.C.

A Clap
of Thunder:

It was the cadence of clattering telegraph keys that brought news of the national events following Abraham Lincoln's 1860 election. By the spring of 1861 Alfred Moore Waddell of Wilmington realized that the biggest story in the history of the republic was about to break. Waddell, whose roots were set deep into the lands of the Cape Fear, had purchased Talcott Burr's *Herald* during what he termed "the flush days" of antebellum prosperity. Waddell wrote:

> On the evening of April 10, 1861, the telegraph operator at the Wilmington office confidentially communicated to me at the *Herald* office a telegram that had just passed through from General Beauregard at Charleston to Jefferson Davis at Richmond, saying they would open fire on Sumter at 4 a.m. if Major Anderson refused to surrender. Thereupon I hurried to the old Manchester Depot on the other side of the (Cape Fear) River and caught the train for Charleston as it was passing out . . .

A feverish excitement gripped the passengers as the great steam engine puffed toward Charleston. As they neared the city "the heavy report like a clap of thunder" could be clearly heard, followed by "the measured throb of artillery." When the train pulled into the station, Waddell raced to his hotel, found the stairs, and climbed upward to get a view:

> As I stepped into the cupola and looked out on that splendid harbor, there in the center of its gateway to the sea, half wrapped in the morning mists, lay Sumter, and high above its parapets, fluttering in the morning breeze floated proudly and defiantly the Stars and Stripes. In a moment afterwards just above it there was a sudden red flash and a column of smoke, followed by an explosion, and opposite on James Island a corresponding puff floated away on the breeze, and I realized with emotions indescribable that I was looking upon a civil war among my countrymen.

The news traveled fast. The Reverend John L. Prichard, pastor of Wilmington's First Baptist Church, noted in his diary:

> April 13, 1861—Fort Sumter bombarded all night! Everyone is excited. War has commenced; when will it end? Sumter surrendered unconditionally by Major Anderson, commander! Great rejoicing in Wilmington, flag raising, etc.

Nancy Nettles, an observant young lady of Wilmington, recalled: "Groups of men could be seen everywhere talking secession, while the women, congregating in each other's houses, talked about a war they were dreading."

With the secession of the Southern states, including South Carolina, Wilmington's secession faction rejoiced—surely, they believed, North Carolina would be forced to follow South Carolina's lead. John Dillard Bellamy, an ardent secessionist, had financed a huge bonfire and parade to celebrate South Carolina's secession, and deeply resented his peers who advocated the Union. But the actions at Fort Sumter had brought nearly everyone in the Cape Fear to the secession side, or so it seemed.

As the nation moved swiftly toward war, thoughtful men recognized that the time had come to choose sides. Most Southerners believed that their "Cause" was just and that a victory could be swiftly won. Jonathan Worth, a Quaker, who would become governor of North Carolina during Reconstruction, reflected a more sober view. He wrote his son, David Gaston Worth:

> I think the South is committing suicide, but my lot is cast with the South, and being unable to manage the ship, I intend to face the breakers manfully, and go down with my companions.

All over the nation men made their choice. Wilmington-born John Ancrum Winslow elected to stay with the United States Navy: He would become infamous (or famous, depending on one's point of view) when, as commander of the U.S.S. *Kearsage,* he sank the C.S.S. *Alabama.* His brother chose the Confederate side and served as a surgeon billeted to Wilmington.

Even Wilmingtonians who lacked Southern roots or loyalties were forced to take a stance. Some pulled up stakes and left town. Henry Robert Kuhl, a native of Prussia, decided to stay. He wrote, "I liked the place . . . I thought the people worth fighting for."

But most native sons had no difficulty in choosing the Confederate side; it was a deep-rooted response, well-approved by the women of the young Confederacy, although some poor whites grumbled that the war was "a rich man's war," while blacks had no choice to make. For most, however, the war effort was exhilarating. Volunteer companies had been drilling for weeks. The Wilmington Light Infantry, under the command of Captain William Lord deRosset, enjoyed the most prestige. The German Volunteers, composed of all Germans, under the leadership of Captain C. Cornehlsen, was the only organization in North Carolina whose common bond was their national origin. Other companies included the Wilmington Rifle Guards, under Captain O.P. Meares; the Cape Fear Light Infantry, under Captain John L. Hedrick; and the Cape Fear Rifles. These reserves shared the limelight with smaller groups that were in part financed by public subscription—The Cape Fear Riflemen, Cape Fear Light Artillery, Citizens' Horseguards, Wilmington Horse Artillery, and the Mechanic Volunteers. Outside of Wilmington, the Topsail Rifles and the Smithville Guards were organized. Shortly after firing on Fort Sumter many of these home guards merged into the newly organized 30th Regiment of the North Carolina Militia. Their first major task was to take over Fort Caswell and Fort Johnston, the federal forts that guarded the Cape Fear River's entrance. The troops, top-heavy with officers, left Wilmington by steamer and their send-off was a gay one, with ladies lining the riverbank waving handkerchiefs. Official word of North Carolina's secession came shortly thereafter. More companies formed,

J.M. Alden drew this scene of the Mound Battery at Fort Fisher during the Union bombardment in January 1865. The relentless firing was recalled by one Confederate soldier who stated: "The earth was in continuous tremor . . . white sand red with blood." Lithograph published by Endicott and Co., N.Y.

including Company H of the 40th Regiment, which was made up of Irishmen, and Company A of the 41st, known as the Rebel Rangers.

Send-offs required music and two days after North Carolina seceded the *Journal* published "Carolina's Sons Are Ready," which was sung to the tune of "Dixie":

> Our gallant boys are going to battle
> Seeking fame where the cannons rattle
> Look away, Look away, Look away—Cheer the boys!

The *Journal* also reported that of the approximate 10,000 white citizens in New Hanover County, over 1,500 had gone into the field to fight. The local newspapers' advertisements carried notices of sales of Confederate brass buttons, gray cloth, boots, pocket Bibles—the necessities of a departing soldier.

The excitement was contagious and Wilmington was swept up in the momentum. Nancy Nettle's girlish enthusiasm was typical:

> We went to see the soldiers drill every day. Companies were forming, bands playing, people cheering. I had never seen a railway station before then, but we went every day to see the soldiers off. The ladies carried hot coffee and sandwiches and went up and down the cars serving the soldiers, while the children stayed to help cheer and wave hands. . . . Everything was in commotion and I was in great glee, till I went home one day and found Mother preparing Jack to go to Fort Fisher. She tried to persuade him to wait, as he was young, but he had caught the fever and had 'To go fight, bleed, and die' for his country.

Heartrending departures had become commonplace. Good-byes and pledges were exchanged. Those who could afford it visited a photographer so that a picture could be added to a snippet of hair pressed in a locket, travel case, or frame. Letter writing took on greater importance and attained a new eloquence based on the poignance of homesickness and separation.

Alfred P. Gurganious, a 34-year-old New Hanover County farmer, joined the Holly Shelter Volunteers at the war's outset. He regularly wrote his wife, who had been left behind to manage the farm and their six children. One of his letters recalled their last evening together:

> I would give anything I have in this world to see you all one more time. When I lie down at night you are the last object on my mind and the first person on my mind in the morning when I rise. I often think of the evening walks, so lovely, we have taken together and more especially the last walk we took together the evening before I left . . . My heart was breaking with trouble to think it was the last supper we would take together for a time. I send to you the best love I can confer on any person . . . I remain your affectionate husband until death.

Susan Gurganious had joined the ranks of women who served by running the house, business, and helping the war effort. Nancy Nettles remembered that in Wilmington women met daily to make "comfortables and knit socks." They emptied their linen chests for supplies to donate for bedding and "scrapped lint and made bandages for the wounded." Women with land had an especially hard time managing, but New Hanover County had 766 free blacks and 10,332 slaves. Nancy Nettles recalled:

Left: *During the Civil War Louise duBrutz Reston sewed for her babies, ran a big household, made ink from berries to sell to the soldiers, brewed vinegar to take to market, and supervised a large salt works, an industry vital to the Confederacy. After the war she entertained General Lee. After she was widowed, she married Charles Pattison Bolles, builder of Fort Fisher's Battery Bolles. Courtesy, Dr. and Mrs. Charles Graham*
Right: *In 1862 the Myrtle Grove area near Wilmington became the site of the State Salt Works, which was similar to the one depicted here. A windmill on the sound pumped water to boilers heated by huge furnaces. The dried salt was then scraped from the pans, packaged, and distributed. Salt was such an important commodity that men who worked in the salt manufacture were exempt from military service, paid soldiers' wages, and provided with rations. Courtesy, North Carolina State Archives*

Finally all were gone and we were left in care of the Home Guard and the negroes. I do not know how we would have lived without the negroes . . . They not only fed the Southern people but clothed them too.

At Bradley Creek, Maria Louise duBrutz Reston energetically applied herself to the challenge. She picked pokeweed berries to make ink to sell to the soldiers. In addition, she related:

I kept house, attending to the making of butter for the entire family and a good supply for market, did all the sewing for the family making all my babies' pretty clothes . . . I also made gallons of vinegar for market . . .

But her greatest effort went into the supervising of a cottage industry that was beginning to thrive up and down the sounds east of Wilmington.

A number of persons . . . began the making of salt as the supply was running short owing to the Blockade. Mr. Reston built his works just below the house . . . near the water where by the use of a windmill, the salt water supplied the means for making salt. Making the salt was a simple process, the main thing was to keep a steady fire in the furnace and stirring the water as soon as the salt would form, removing the salt to bins for drying and supplying the vats with fresh water. I had . . . eight reliable colored men to do the work, four to tend the salt and four to cut the wood to supply our own works and to supply others who needed wood as we owned a large body of heavily wooded land. I . . . would run down to the salt works four and five times a day and on Friday have the salt packed in

large boxes to be sent to market, sewing up all the bags myself and keeping account of the number of bags sent up. We had ready sales for salt and ink and money came in freely . . .

Salt making was not new to the region, but during the war years it burgeoned into one of the Lower Cape Fear's most important industries, which fattened the local economy. It took so many trees to fuel the fires that burned through the night that forest land along the sounds was depleted. Not only did the sounds support many private salt works, such as the one the enterprising Restons maintained, but Myrtle Grove Sound became the site of the State Salt Works, which operated on a grand scale during the war.

In 1861 Dr. John Milton Worth was elected State Salt Commissioner; later he was replaced by his nephew, David Gaston Worth. The Worths supervised a recruiting effort to hire workers, both black and white, who were exempted from military service, paid soldiers' wages, and provided rations. The commissioner was also responsible for production management (in a good month 5,000 pounds could be produced), and he enforced the government controls regulating production and distribution.

As Louise Reston had observed, it was the Union blockade at the entrance of the Cape Fear River that made the production of salt such a vital industry to Wilmington and the Confederacy. When President Lincoln proclaimed a blockade of the South's ports in 1861, he set into motion a series of events that dramatically altered the lives of the people of the Lower Cape Fear.

REBEL SALT WORKS, MOREHEAD CITY, NORTH CAROLINA.—FROM A SKETCH BY OUR SPECIAL ARTIST, MR. SCHELL.—SEE PAGE 890.

The Cape Fear River provided entry to the port of Wilmington where three railroads led out to the South's interior. The Wilmington and Weldon Railroad led through Petersburg to Richmond and served as the lifeline to General Robert E. Lee's Army of Northern Virginia. Lincoln wanted that lifeline cut and he sought to establish an effective Union blockade of Southern ports, which would prevent the import of basic necessities and starve the South into submission. However, a blockade was easier to proclaim than to achieve.

When *Daylight,* the first Union blockader, arrived on June 20, 1861, it was easy to perceive the difficult assignment that lay before her. Commodore (later Admiral) David Dixon Porter, USN, commanded the squadron, a motley collection of sailing frigates, converted paddlewheel steamers, tugboats, ferryboats, schooners, sloops, ships, and barques. The Union strategists had assumed they could easily situate a crescent-shaped cordon off Cape Fear which could vigilantly patrol to prevent entry and exit from the river, but they had forgotten what mariners had discovered centuries before—this was the Cape known as Fear. Geography was on the side of the Confederacy. Not only did 20 miles of the treacherous Frying Pan Shoals spew out to sea from the river's mouth, but there were two river entrances—one on the northeast at New Inlet, and one on the southwest at Smith (Bald Head) Island. This meant the blockaders either had to divide up and patrol the two entries, or run a 40-mile chase around those tricky shoals, which were poorly charted.

The best of charts would have been a poor match for the knowledge of the Smithville pilots who had spent a lifetime mastering the course of safe channel. These pilots worked in tandem with the runner captains—intrepid sailors who were sometimes "off-leave" Confederate or British naval officers. (Officers who were "off-leave" took an unauthorized leave of absence to cash in on the lucrative blockade-running business.) Together the pilot and captain counted on a fast ship, sure knowledge of the sea and sand beneath them, the right tide, a waning moon, instinct, and daring to carry them through the blockade. It was a risky business—between November 1861 and March 1862, of the 425 known attempts to run the blockade, 363 were successful.

The Confederacy placed a high priority on the Port of Wilmington. Fort Fisher and batteries on Zeke's Island guarded New Inlet, while Fort Caswell, Fort Holmes, Battery Campbell, and Battery Shaw guarded Old Inlet—plus there was a garrison fort, Fort Johnston, at Smithville, and a second line of defense at Fort Anderson at old Brunswick Town. In April 1861 Captain Charles Pattison Bolles had been assigned to construct sand batteries overlooking New Inlet, initiating the construction of the huge earthenworks fortress later known as Fort Fisher. Later Colonel William Lamb took over the supervision of the fort's erection, which was based on a composite of plans designed by General William Chase Whiting (who became the officer in charge of the Cape Fear's defenses), R.G. Pittman, Bolles, Lamb, and others. Hundreds of slaves, who were relieved at harvest time by poor whites who had been conscripted for service, dug sand, placed logs into pits, covered them with sand, and reinforced them with palmetto fronds. Gradually the massive fort took shape. Heat, humidity, sand flies, and monotony all took their toll on those who labored. The Lamb family lightened the load by taking an interest in the soldiers who shared the isolation of the garrison at

Admiral David Dixon Porter was given command of the North Atlantic Blockading Squadron in October 1864 for the express purpose of closing the port of Wilmington and its supply line to the outside world. Porter is pictured here in the fall of 1864 on board his flagship, the U.S.S. Malvern. Courtesy, North Carolina State Archives

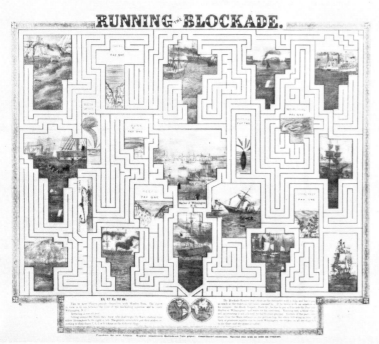

RUNNING THE BLOCKADE.

Above: *The Northern press delighted in lampooning the Confederacy in cartoons. This one depicts the Confederacy as a scorpion engulfed by superior Union might afloat and ashore. Part of the original caption read: "When cornered, and no avenue of escape appearing, it usually stings itself to death — striking its poisonous sting into its own head, which is the softest and consequently most vulnerable part of its body." Of course, the South did not share this assessment.*

Left: *This 19th-century board game suggests some of the hazards blockade runners might have encountered before reaching Wilmington, home, and the center of the board. There were waterspouts, whirlpools, sharks, coral reefs, torpedoes and the ever-present Union Blockade. Courtesy, New Hanover County Museum*

windswept Fort Fisher, but it was the daily drama on the waters below the fort that gave the best respite.

Major James Stevenson had built a log house at the fort for his family, including his sister-in-law, Mary Saunders. She recalled: "I became so accustomed to the sound of booming cannon and exploding shells that I paid no more attention to them than the puffing steamers plying our river." One day she was startled to see that in broad daylight *The Little Hattie* was about to run the blockade. With binoculars she watched in fear, for aboard the runner was her nephew, Daniel S. Stevenson. As *Hattie* made a dash for it, Mary saw a Confederate flag hoisted up the staff. Her nephew later told her that when Captain Lebby realized he'd been spotted and that he would have to make the dash, he had the fires stoked with Nassau bacon for greater speed, ordered the flag raised, and rallied his crew with the cry, "If we must die, we will die game!"

Many died in Wilmington in the late summer and fall of 1862, but the harbinger of death that year was more stealthy than cannonball. Whenever the story of Wilmington's yellow fever epidemic is told it begins with, "The little steamer *Kate* out of Nassau . . ." Supposedly, it was this vessel that brought the fever to Wilmington, an accounting of the epidemic's origins that began with an editorial written by James Fulton in his *Journal*. The story has persisted despite the fact that Edwin Alexander Anderson, M.D. and William T. Wragg, M.D., physicians who treated yellow fever victims during the epidemic, both published papers in respected medical journals refuting the *Kate* story. They concluded that of the 10 doctors who were present in Wilmington during the epidemic, none had ever seen or treated yellow fever and so did not recognize the symptoms when the epidemic was in its embryonic stage. Yellow fever's symptoms soon became all too familiar. Its onset was usually sudden and might be accompanied by chills. For the first two days the victim suffered headache, backache, plus fever. A flushed face, nausea, and vomiting followed. As the fever increased, the pulse decreased. Sometimes the "yellow" of the disease, jaundice, appeared, followed by stomach and intestinal hemorrhages, which caused the dread "black vomit." This stage was followed by either recovery or death.

In 1862 no one recognized the mosquito as the carrier of the disease, but the hot humid months had always been considered the "sickly season." September 1862 was a most sickly season, but at the beginning the presence of an epidemic was stoutly denied by Wilmington authorities. The mayor published an official notice stating there was no cause for alarm, but people's eyes told them differently. Soon John Dillard Bellamy, Jr. could stand on the steps of his father's mansion to watch "the wagon loads of corpses" going out Market Street to Oakdale Cemetery.

People believed an epidemic could be smoked out, so rosin fires burned all over the city. When William T. Wragg, M.D., the Confederate government's official medical representative to the afflicted city, disembarked from his train in Wilmington he immediately noticed the dense black smoke canopy that hung overhead. It seemed a malevolent symbol of the suffering beneath it.

Those who could fled Wilmington but physicians and ministers stayed behind. One of the town's most beloved doctors, James Henderson Dickson, M.D. worked around the clock to keep up with the many calls. Eventually he realized that he had contracted the fever himself; he gave final instructions to his patients, and went home to die.

Relief was ecumenical: Jewish Wilmingtonians who had fled to Charlotte collected funds for the afflicted. The Sisters of Mercy, a Roman Catholic nursing order, arrived from Charleston to nurse the victims. The Reverend Robert B. Drane of St. James Church (Episcopal), Father Murphy of St. Thomas the Apostle Catholic Church, and the Reverend John L. Prichard of the First Baptist Church visited the sick, read the Bible, administered communion, and prayed for the dead until each was too sick to carry on—all three died.

As the weeks wore on Wilmington became more isolated in its suffering. James Fulton had struggled to keep the *Journal* going, but he became too exhausted, and closed down. The telegraph service was terminated. Other towns banned refugees from Wilmington. Mr. Quiqley, superintendent of Oakdale Cemetery, died. Accurate cemetery records were no longer kept and a pit was dug for mass burial of the fever victims.

Finally in November the long heat spell broke and the epidemic ended with the first frost. The Reverend A. Paul Repiton, who had also served the sick throughout the seige, announced that a service "Of Humiliation and Thanksgiving" would be offered at the Orange Street Baptist Church "without regards to sects." The salt commissioner, David Gaston Worth, informed Governor Vance: "There are no traces of yellow fever left." When the staggering statistics were tallied they showed that 654 had died, almost a third of Wilmington's population. Those who survived regained their strength, put their houses in order, and tried to face the adversities of their wartime existence.

The link to the outside world—the telegraph—was reinstated. People were hungry for good news to help lift the shroud of despair that engulfed them. They were amazed to learn that while Wilmington had been held in the vise of yellow fever, so had Lieutenant John Newland Maffitt, while aboard his ship, the C.S.S. *Florida*; and that Maffitt had roused from his fever to take the *Florida*, which was unarmed, into Mobile Bay, where he tricked the Union squadron patrolling it and sailed brazenly into Mobile. There he outfitted his ship, evaded the blockade again, and slipped out to sea under the cover of darkness.

This news gave the Confederacy a naval hero and Wilmington was proud to claim him as its own. Maffitt had grown up near Fayetteville, but his family and friends had close Wilmington connections. He had served in the U.S. Navy and spent 14 years as a hydrographer taking soundings of the coastlines (many in the Lower Cape Fear). With the outbreak of the war he resigned his commission and reported to President Davis for an assignment. As the Confederacy had not yet organized its navy, he took up blockade running and his intimate knowledge of the Lower Cape Fear served him well.

Whenever his ship came through the Cape Fear blockade, Maffitt would hold court in his cabin at Wilmington's docks. His rum punch was legendary and the ladies found it fascinating that he was a real "son of Neptune"—he had actually been born at sea in 1819. His biographers labeled him "The Sea Devil of the Confederacy," for he was the only Confederate naval officer to successfully play two daring roles—that of blockade runner and commerce raider who destroyed more than 55 ships.

While Maffitt earned the sobriquet "Prince of Blockade Runners," there were others whose feats merited plaudits. The average blockade runner made only four successful runs, so anyone who could outwit the law of averages became a hero. John Wilkinson, who made 21 runs aboard the *R.E. Lee*, Captain Lebby, and Charles Hobart-Hampton, who used a variety of aliases, including "Captain Roberts," all became famous. Vessels also earned reputations, among them North Carolina's *Advance*; the *Siren*, which was credited with 64 runs; the infamous *Kate*; and the *Lilian*, whose young purser, James Sprunt, was taken captive. Sprunt later published his recollections of blockade-running as *Tales of the Cape Fear Blockade* and *Derelicts*. His exciting, true-life stories made fascinating reading and two popular stories involved plucky women who ran the blockade.

Mrs. Louis H. deRosset and her infant daughter, Gabrielle, boarded the *Lynx* at Wilmington to go to Nassau, where her husband (an agent of the Confederacy who had successfully run the blockade) lay ill with yellow fever. At New Inlet the vessel was detected and attacked; as the boat began to take on water, Mrs. deRosset handed her child to a sailor, jumped overboard, managed to obtain a firm footing in the shallow water and had her baby tossed to her. She succeeded in escaping, and the commandant of Fort Fisher sent a mule-drawn cart which brought her to the fort. From there she returned to Wilmington. Not long after this incident, she boarded Captain Maffitt's *Tallahassee* and this time successfully ran the blockade. She got to Nassau and nursed her husband back to health.

Rose O'Neal Greenhow had run the blockade on several occasions as "Rebel Rose," a Confederate courier and secret agent. She had paid for her activities by serving time in Washington's Capitol Prison. After her release she went abroad where she regained her health and collected money for the Confederacy. In 1864 she left England aboard the *Condor*, with the famous "Captain Roberts" as commander. She had many dispatch cases and a leather pouch filled with gold which she always wore around her neck. Off Cape Fear the *Condor* ran into heavy seas. Mrs. Greenhow panicked in fear that they would capsize and seemed terrified that she would be recaptured by the Union blockade fleet and returned to prison. Captain Roberts tried to convince her that the *Condor* could ride out the storm but she could not be pacified, and finally, a dinghy was lowered for the strong-willed Mrs. Greenhow. Almost at once the small boat capsized and Rebel Rose was washed away, the heavy gold an anchor around her neck. Her body was found on the beach near Fort Fisher, then taken to Wilmington where she was buried at Oakdale Cemetery with full military honors.

Although Wilmington's citizens suffered many deprivations because of the blockade, there were also tremendous profits being made by speculators. As Captain Wilkinson wrote in *Harper's Magazine*: "The staid old town of Wilmington was turned topsy-turvy by the war."

Cotton from all over the Confederacy was shipped to Wilmington and cotton compresses ran 24 hours a day. Cotton was bought cheap and loaded into the holds of specially designed low-freeboard craft, powered by mighty steam engines that were fueled by an almost smokeless coal. The ships were painted the leaden gray of overcast skies so as to be almost invisible. When the tide and moon were right, the runners would travel the 28 nautical miles down the Cape Fear River, and, under the cover of Confederate guns, make the

With the realization that war was inevitable, men all over the nation were forced to choose sides. John Newland Maffitt resigned his commission in the United States Navy and reported to President Jefferson Davis for assignment. Courtesy, North Carolina State Archives

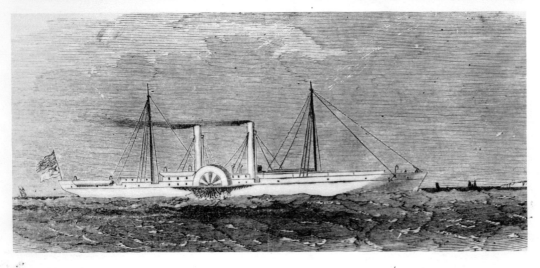

Above: In 1864 Union blockaders on station off Wilmington at Old Inlet patrolled the southern passage into the Cape Fear River. Old Inlet was protected by Fort Caswell and Smith's Island Battery. Courtesy, North Carolina State Archives

Left: Meanwhile, at New Inlet Union blockaders patrolled the northeast passage into the Cape Fear River. New Inlet was protected by Fort Fisher (seen in the background). From the North Carolina Collection, UNC Library, Chapel Hill

Left: Blockade runners took advantage of moonless nights and rising tides to dash through the blockade to the safety of Confederate guns. Lieutenant Commander John Wilkinson, C.S.N., made 21 successful trips on the Robert E. Lee, the vessel pictured here. Courtesy, North Carolina State Archives

Right: Confederate heroine Rose O'Neal Greenhow, agent and courier, paid for her beliefs by serving time in Washington's Capitol Prison. She gave her life while running the blockade near Wilmington and is buried in Oakdale Cemetery. Courtesy, Historic St. Thomas Preservation Society, Inc.

run to open seas. They would then head for Nassau 570 miles away, or go the 654 miles to Bermuda. In these islands the cotton was unloaded and sold for enormous profits—sometimes it was bought for 3 cents a pound and sold for a $1 a pound. The speculator, the captain, and even the lowliest seaman all got rich—a quarter of a million dollars could be made in one run; the captain could clear as much as $5,000. In the islands the ships would be refilled with necessary goods for the Confederacy plus irresistable luxuries, which had a ready market when the ships returned to Wilmington—they then headed back across the sea for the dash through the blockade. Everyone breathed more easily when safe anchorage was made at Smithville where the pilot would take leave to be with his family. The next morning the jubilant captain would head upstream to Wilmington where his much-heralded arrival brought whoops, hollers, and drinks all around, followed by auctions where luxuries went to the highest bidder. Big money created instant inflation: a ham cost $50; flour, $500 a barrel; and coffee, $100 a pound. Those who were not involved in the speculation or who were not employed on a fixed salary struggled to survive while the profiteers swilled champagne.

As a port town, Wilmington had always had its share of the seamy element, but no one was quite prepared for the bawdy ostentation that went on during the years of blockade running. Many citizens chose to seek the quiet haven of "the back country," staying with family and friends, while the town's population swelled with those who had come to get rich quick. The City Hotel, The Globe House, and the Palmetto House had no rooms for let. The big spenders leased vacant houses and little boys sneaked up at night to steal a peak through the blinds at all the goings-on inside, from cockfights to striptease. Gamblers, prostitutes, and swindlers paraded in the streets, and the blockade auctions attracted noisy crowds of flashy speculators whose manners were rougher than the diamonds in their silk cravats.

Spin-off profits filtered down to improve some phases of the local economy. In 1863 the Wilmington and Weldon Railroad quadrupled its dividend, bank dividends increased, almost every store in town handled local salt, and industries geared to the war effort: the Confederate Sword Company, and a fishery that used fish oil to waterproof blankets, tents, and uniforms made money, as did the shipyards.

Benjamin Washington Beery, who had learned the shipbuilding trade in Baltimore, and his brother William purchased the Cape Fear Marine Railway in 1861. By 1864 more than 150 employees were at work at the shipyard known as the Navy Yard or Confederate Shipyard: many were detailed from the Navy and did double duty by sleeping with their rifles beside them at the Courthouse at night. There the Beerys built the ironclad ram, C.S.S. *North Carolina.* Their competitors, the Cassidey brothers, built a similar ironclad, C.S.S. *Raleigh.*

Despite the exodus of civilians, enough people remained in town to keep its institutions functioning. Most churches continued services, and schools were in session. The nearby military garrisons provided attractive men who enjoyed Wilmington's hospitality when they were on furlough. New Hanover County issued 411 marriage licenses during the war years. The war spawned humanitarian efforts, as spiraling inflation had created some dreadful problems. John Allan Taylor chaired the Town Wardens of the Poor Committee, while the Wilmington Relief Association collected food. The Committee of

Safety, the Sanitary Committee, and the Seamen's Friends Society also solicited funds for the impoverished.

Three railroads to Wilmington made the town an important stopover for soldiers, and trainloads of wounded came through on a regular basis. Mrs. Armand John deRosset, one of the town's wealthiest matrons, earned quite a reputation for her work on behalf of the military through the Soldiers' Aid Society. All the ladies in the group lobbied rich speculators and blockade runners for donations of cash and luxury treats to give to the soldiers at the Wayside House they had established where soldiers could rest, eat, and wash. One grateful recipient wrote the *Journal* to express his thanks and noted, "I have heard many soldiers speak of the kind treatment from the kind ladies of Wilmington."

Miss Mary Ann Buie became famous for her soldier relief work, but she created controversy since in those days an outspoken, liberated female college graduate who badgered people on the street for donations was considered an eccentric. However, her persistence got results—she wrote Governor Vance that she had raised half a million dollars' worth of supplies, and her philanthropy endeared her to the soldiers in camp who gave her the name "the Soldiers' Friend." The troops at Fort Fisher collected $135, which they sent to Miss Buie, with the request that she use it to buy Christmas dinner for the sick soldiers in Wilmington. But the Union fleet had different plans for Wilmington's 1864 Christmas.

Since October, rumors had circulated that Union strategists believed they must shut down the Confederacy's last port, Wilmington, so that the supply route to Lee's army could be destroyed. Everyone knew that an assault on Fort Fisher was inevitable, although there was no particular panic. Wilmington believed the massive fort, which had been compared to the famed Maldkoff of the Crimean War, could withstand anything the Union chose to throw at it. Local people also had confidence in the abilities of General Whiting and Colonel Lamb, but this confidence was shaken when the terse announcement came that Whiting would be demoted to second in command to be replaced by General Braxton Bragg. It didn't help morale when a Richmond newspaper warned, "Braxton Bragg has been ordered to Wilmington, Good Bye Wilmington!" On December 20, rumor turned to reality; Admiral David Dixon Porter's Union fleet appeared on the horizon off Fort Fisher, but a strong gale and heavy seas forced them too far off shore to be able to attack. Colonel Lamb sent the slaves to Wilmington and at the forts, in town, and in the countryside everyone waited.

The weather cleared on the 23rd. Union General Benjamin F. Butler had devised a scheme whereby the U.S.S. *Louisiana* would be filled with 300 tons of powder, towed under cover of darkness to the shallow waters about 200 yards from the fort's parapet base, and blown up—knocking out the fort in the explosion. At 1:45 a.m. the *Louisiana* exploded as planned, but the fort held firm and Lamb

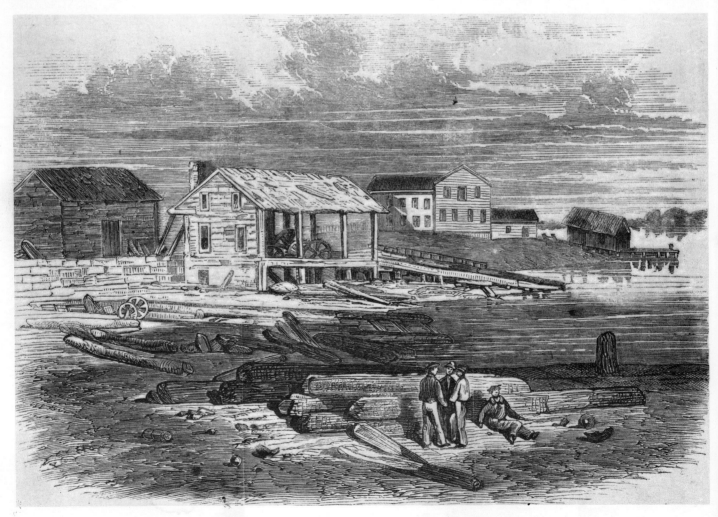

noted in his journal, "A blockader got aground near the fort, set a fire to herself and blew up." His memory of what followed:

> Saturday, December 24th, was one of those perfect winter days that occasionally are experienced in the latitude of the Cape Fear . . . the air was balmy for winter, and the sun shone . . . and the deep blue sea was as calm as a lake and broke lazily on the bar and beach. A grander sight than the approach of Porter's formidable Armada towards the fort was never witnessed on our coast. With the rising sun out of the old ocean there came upon the horizon one after another the vessels of the fleet, the grand frigate leading the van followed by the iron clads. More than fifty men-of-war heading for the Confederate stronghold. At nine o'clock the men were beat to quarters and silently the detachments stood by their guns. On the vessels came, growing larger and more imposing as the distance lessened between them and the resolute men who defended their homes.

Then at 11:30 a.m. the signal was given and the bombardment began. At one point the garrison flag was shot away and Private Christopher C. Bland climbed up the staff twice under heavy fire to repair the flag to the halyard. At 5:30 p.m. the bombardment ended. Fort Fisher fired a final salvo as an affirmation that they were still operative. At 10 a.m. on Christmas Day the bombardment resumed. While shells rained upon the fort the people in Wilmington experienced an unforgettable day—windows rattled with each explosion and the terrifying sound of the bombardment was almost deafening. The very air seemed singed with gunpowder. At St. James the congregation knelt to recite the familiar litany: "Good Lord Deliver Us." In many houses Christmas dinner was served, but countless diaries reveal that many a woman excused herself to retire to a private spot to weep or pray for the troops under attack. Many of those troops were North Carolinians so the attack seemed especially personal. Some of the younger set found the pyrotechnics exhilarating. One group of boys raced to the First Baptist Church at Fifth and Market where the unfinished steeple provided a ladder up to the sky; one daredevil climbed to the bell tower and declared he could see the whole battle and proceeded to relay a graphic description to those below. At 5:30 p.m. the windows stopped shaking. News was telegraphed to Dr. deRosset's house at Third and Market, which was Confederate headquarters, that the Union fleet had withdrawn. Later it was reported that General Butler's Union soldiers had advanced to within 75 yards of the fort but had then been ordered to retreat. Lamb reported that the fortress and 1,371 men had withstood a barage of attack "certainly never surpassed in warfare" before then.

This repulse brought a euphoria to the Confederacy. But there was little time for the Confederacy to savor this sweet victory as everyone anticipated a renewed assault. Colonel Lamb wrote: "I sent dear wife and children across the river." Many evacuated Wilmington to refuge in places considered more secure. The year 1865 rang in mournfully. Warfront news had become grim and supplies were running low. ◆ ◆ ◆

Beery and Cassidy shipyards supplied the Confederacy with vessels, including ironclads. Both were dismantled or destroyed after the fall of Fort Fisher to keep them from falling into the hands of the advancing Union troops. This engraving from Frank Leslie's Illustrated Newspaper *shows the ruins of the Rebel Navy Yard at Wilmington. Courtesy, Naval Historical Center*

The Union fleet returned the night of January 12 and on the next morning the bombardment began. This time it was more accurate and concentrated and the land face of Fort Fisher received unabated shelling. Before the day was out Chase Whiting, who was known as "Little Billy" among the soldiers, arrived voluntarily to be with Lamb; he told him, "You and your garrison are to be sacrificed" and reported that Bragg was looking for another place to fall back upon. When dusk fell the bombardment did not cease as it had in December, but continued through the night. One witness guiltily admitted he found an awesome beauty in the bursting rockets that lit the night. Henry Clay MacQueen remembered: "Three days and they kept up the ceaseless firing. The ocean seemed covered with gunboats and transports bearing soldiers. We had not time to eat, or be relieved from duty or bury the dead. The earth was in continuous tremor . . . white sand red with blood."

On January 15 the firing shifted to the sea face. Shrill steam whistles blew in unison as the signal to charge, and the huge amphibious land force north of Fort Fisher advanced on the garrison. Colonel Lamb fell wounded. Wilmington's Major James Reilly took command of the battle, which had been reduced to hand-to-hand combat. As the hours wore on the Union force gained ground. At 10 p.m. the Union announced they had taken Fort Fisher—the ships off shore responded with whistles and fireworks, and those left behind in Wilmington read the sky and knew they were lost. At Military Hospital No. 11 Richard P. Paddison wrote: "The Yankees took Fort Fisher and last night our troops blew up all the forts below that point. I think this is the hardest blow the Confederacy has yet received." The Union had paid a high price for its success and the Confederate army had suffered about 500 casualties with 1,400 taken prisoner. Fort Anderson held out until February 19, but the retreat had been sounded. Captain John W. Taylor wrote in his pocket diary:

> Marched all day, Fought all day. Evacuated Town Creek Bridge through a torrent of shell and arrived in Wilmington, 1 P.M. 21 Feb., evacuated Wilmington the 22nd, heavy skirmishes all night . . . marched to Burgaw.

Union forces found it symbolic that they should "liberate" Wilmington on George Washington's birthday. J. Warren Poland aboard the U.S.S. *Nyack* wrote to his mother as the vessel steamed up the Cape Fear River:

> . . . We are having a day of jubilee today . . . The rebels have been burning cotton, rosin, etc. and for two days . . . black smoke has risen from the doomed city . . . In a few days you will hear of the capture of [Wilmington] We can see the church spires of the city and it is rumored she has surrendered. Shall I bring you a silk dress from W.? This is a splendid day, clear and warm as June . . . I am very glad to be here at the surrender and it will repay me for all the privations I have endured. . . . Here we are within 2 rods of the city. On the right is the ruins of the government store house that was filled with cotton but is now all burnt out. On the other side was a large factory the rebs burnt . . . the city contains many brick and some handsome homes. The inhabitants are very shabby and no wonder for they have been under the Devil's rule. The darkies are running around delighted at "massa Lincoln's coming" and at the prospect of being Free. I shall ever remember this day and I had rather work a year without pay, than miss being here . . .

Most of Wilmington's white population would not have

This page, top: *On January 13, 1865, Union troops guarded by Admiral Porter's fleet landed by transport to storm Fort Fisher. It was only a matter of time before the mighty fortress fell. Courtesy, U.S. Naval Historical Center*
Middle: *When the fall of Wilmington was imminent, Confederates sank ships and other obstructions to hamper Union progress up the Cape Fear River. The artist for this engraving, sitting at the tip of Point Peter, watched as sailors from Admiral Porter's fleet removed the debris. Courtesy, Mrs. Leslie N. Boney, Jr.*
Bottom: *Fort Fisher had taken hundreds of laborers four years to build and was believed to be impregnable. This photo was taken shortly after the fortress succumbed to the gunfire of Admiral Porter's huge fleet. From the Brady Collection, National Archives. Courtesy, Lower Cape Fear Historical Society*
Facing page: *Many North Carolina blacks took an active part in the war that was to bring them freedom from slavery. Thousands joined the Union Army, and subsequently served as medical aides, spies, recruiters, laborers, and soldiers. Courtesy, North Carolina State Archives*

understood Poland's jubilation, but they did understand that their defenses had been destroyed. Catherine deRosset Meares wrote in a letter:

> Darkness and gloom cover us like a pall. These immense fires on each side of town were fearful. Contrary winds blew the dense black smoke directly toward town and when the heavy black clouds met at the center, it seemed as if a dark, oppressive girdle (typical of our future) encompassed the town . . .

John Dawson had served as mayor throughout the years of adversity. It was now his deepest wish that no more harm come to Wilmington's citizens. He grimly walked to City Hall to await the conquerors.

What would follow next? For some people curiosity outweighed fright and they went out to the streets to see. In the throng was the Reverend L.S. Burkhead, pastor of the Front Street Methodist Church. Soon the Union army came into view. He remembered:

> Then came General Terry at the head of the column up Front Street, with the strains of martial music, and colors flying, leaving the main column at Market Street, heading a squadron of splendidly equipped men mounted on superb chargers — every horse a beautiful bay — he dashed up to City Hall.

There Mayor Dawson formally surrendered.

As the Union parade continued to cross from Eagles' Island, townspeople pushed forward to see these Yankees. One group identified themselves as a company from Kentucky, which sent a glimmer of hope among the crowd that perhaps those with a speaking acquaintance with ham and biscuits might be more kindhearted than Northern Yankees. As the parade ended, voices were heard in the distance. The song "The Battle Hymn of the Republic" grew louder and it was soon obvious that those singing were companies of black Union soldiers. The blacks in the crowd reacted with joyful hysteria. The whites became stony-faced — one white-haired gentleman threw his arms to the sky and loudly implored as he looked upward, "Blow Gabriel, blow, for God's sake blow!"

As Brother Burkhead walked away from the parade he wondered if the black members of his congregation really understood the implications of what had just transpired. He pondered over the text of his next morning's sermon so that he could give his flock, particularly his "black sheep," proper counsel. The next morning when he got to church for the blacks' service he noticed that one of his congregation had begun the reading; the text was Psalm IX:

> I will be glad and rejoice . . .
> When my enemies are turned back, they shall fall and perish
> Thou has destroyed the wicked

As Burkhead watched he saw that his "whole congregation was wild with excitement, and extravagant beyond all precedent with shouts, groans, Amens, and unseemly demonstrations." No longer did he wonder whether his "black sheep" understood the implications. All he feared had come true and he went home to pray.

General Joseph Roswell Hawley, a native of North Carolina and an ardent abolitionist, took over Wilmington. He commandeered the Bellamy Mansion as his headquarters, and once more Market Street became the address of an enemy commander.

◆ ◆ ◆

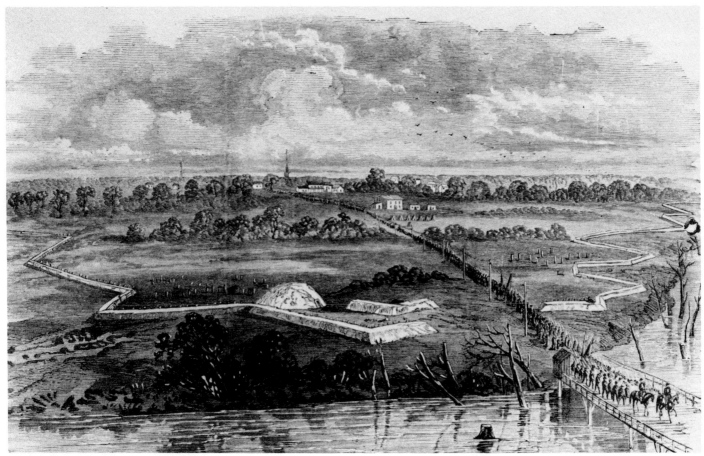

Facing page, top: *After the fall of Fort Fisher General Terry positioned himself about three miles above the fort with the Union Fleet in both the river on his left and the ocean on his right. Here he could keep a keen eye on Confederate activities in the Lower Cape Fear. Courtesy, North Carolina State Archives*

Bottom: *In March 1865, after the fall of Wilmington, General Schofield's army began its march northwards toward New Bern, leaving behind Wilmington and the now useless and abandoned Confederate defenses. They are pictured here (in an exaggerated drawing) crossing Green's Mill Pond (known now as Burnt Mill Creek) with Wilmington in the background. Courtesy, North Carolina State Archives*

This page, top: *There was rejoicing when black troops under the command of General Wild began liberating slaves in North Carolina. They were now emancipated and they looked to the Freedman's Bureau for their new direction.*

Bottom: *After the fall of Wilmington Union forces sent Captain Ainsworth steaming up the Cape Fear River toward Fayetteville to open communications with General Sherman. From the North Carolina Collection, UNC Library, Chapel Hill*

Bad Times, Good Times, New Times:

If the war turned Wilmington "topsy-turvy," Reconstruction pulled it inside out. No one even quite knew how to refer to the war, which had concluded with the South's surrender two months after Wilmington's. The U.S. Government chose to imprint on its official 30-volume account of the war: The War of the Rebellion. Confederate veterans recalled the War of Northern Aggression or the War for Southern Independence. Ladies preferred euphemisms: The Late Unpleasantness or the Conflict. By whatever name, *The War* had indelibly marked the lives and attitudes of those who survived it.

Grim statistics revealed North Carolina had lost 40,000 men. Fields lay fallow, farms and livestock had been destroyed, businesses had been burnt out, banks had failed, Confederate money was worthless, and the social system lay in chaos. If a family had escaped loss or hardship, or enjoyed a profit during the war years, they were loath to admit it. For many of the gentility, poverty became a badge of honor.

As the news trickled home relating the story of the final hours before Fort Fisher fell, of Chase Whiting's death at Governor's Island, of the valiant last North Carolina stand at Bentonville, or of the solemn dignity of Appomattox, even the most stoical wept.

One by one the soldiers returned home. Alfred Gurganious, the soldier who had written his wife, "I would give everything I have in this world to see you all one more time" left the Confederate hospital in Richmond, walked all the way home, and died two days later. Colonel John D. Taylor proved his valor at Bentonville and returned home with one uniform sleeve empty. James Alexander Montgomery had enlisted at age 17 and served under Colonel Taylor at Fort Fisher. When the fort fell, Montgomery was sent as a prisoner-of-war to Point Lookout, Maryland, where he shivered "in the coldest place in the world" under one thin blanket. Upon release he wrote:

> I rode on top of the box cars to Wilmington. The Virginia fronts were pink with redbud and every ditchbank white with alder. When I got to Wilmington, I was ragged and dirty and covered with vermin, shoes hardly held to my feet. I slept in a butcher's stall in the market house. I had had nothing to eat for four days and nights, but stumbled on twelve miles to my home on Myrtle Grove Sound.

Many walked all the way home. Sergeant Benjamin Franklin Hall and a friend started home from Appomattox. Some Union soldiers offered them a lift, but the proud Rebel replied, "No, we've walked this far, we'll finish on foot." Wilmingtonians were heartened by the stories that told of the valor and tenacity of their men. George Davis had served the Confederacy well as a senator and as attorney general. When he returned home to reopen his law practice, he was often stopped on the street by those who wanted to shake his hand. There was parochial pride too in Judah Benjamin, who served the Confederacy as secretary of war, secretary of state, and attorney general.

William MacRae returned home to find he had become a local hero. He began his military career as a private and ended it as a brigadier-general—and a veteran of some of the war's most famous battles. As commander of the brigade that covered the retreat at Farmville, Virginia, he had been with the last group of Confederates to lay down their arms. All eight of the MacRae brothers had fought in the war—seven in gray, one in blue.

Despite Lee's surrender in April 1865, civilians as well as soldiers displayed their continuing loyalty to the Confederacy. Old Doctor Thomas Fanning Wood—founder of the North Carolina Board of Health and *North Carolina Medical Journal,* and botanist of local renown—refused to tend patients unless he be allowed to wear his Confederate uniform. The Reverend Alfred Augustus Watson, rector of St. James, continued to pray for Jefferson Davis at his Sunday services; an infuriated General Joseph R. Hawley of the occupational forces had the St. James' pews thrown into the street and converted the church to a Union hospital, lending credibility to the stories that circulated of occupational forces' theft, desecration, and destruction of private property. It particularly rankled that the First Presbyterian Church Bible was stolen.

Oaths of allegiance to the restored federal authority were required and while most people wished to defy that authority, they also had to survive. John Davis Robbins, Jr. remembered:

> The family was left without anything to eat and after three weeks of starving with nothing but oysters to subsist on, Mrs. Robbins very reluctantly went across the Cape Fear River and took the oath.

The war's end caused thousands of refugees to seek out Wilmington for sanctuary. Ironically, many of Wilmington's residents had fled to "the back country." General William Tecumseh Sherman had written Admiral Porter on December 31, 1864 that he planned to march through the Carolinas "tearing up roads and smashing things generally" and take Wilmington from the rear. Sherman's plans changed, but as he progressed on his long march, "smashing things generally," refugees scurried ahead of him. Whites were joined by thousands of freed blacks who crowded the approaches into town. The *Herald* reported that the refugees were "a most wretched and pitiable" sight. General Hawley, who had no reputation for softheartedness, wrote his wife, "I stood dumb before the great misery."

The black refugees trudged toward Wilmington in hopeful expectation. They had been emancipated and now expected the Freedmen's Bureau to fulfill their expectations. For many, sweetness had become equated with a dessert of the poor—molasses. Throughout those bewildering days while black refugees choked the roads, there were reports that they could be heard crooning the popular spiritual of the Lower Cape Fear, which contained the repeating refrain—"De Angels pouring 'lasses down."

But for white Wilmingtonians, Reconstruction was a bitter pill to swallow. Even the federal government's policy of amnesty

In 1894 John Van B. Metts looked splendid in the green and gold dress uniform of the Wilmington Light Infantry. Organized in 1853 as a "Uniform Volunteer Company of Infantry," the Wilmington Light Infantry was an outgrowth of the colonial militia. In 1861 the company was one of four in the region. There also existed the Wilmington Rifle Guards, the German Volunteers, and the Cape Fear Light Infantry. Courtesy, Mrs. Spotswood H. Huntt

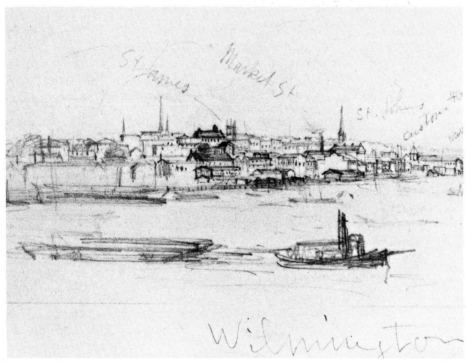

This page, top: *Nineteenth-century smugglers sometimes sought refuge in the secluded creeks that emptied in the sounds. In 1867 Harper's Pictorial illustrated these brigands whose fate was a grave at the bottom of Masonboro Sound. From the North Carolina Collection, UNC Library, Chapel Hill*

Middle and Bottom: *Alfred R. Waud was one of the most famous 19th-century illustrators in America. Few people, however, saw Waud's original drawings since printing presses of the time were incapable of reproducing them exactly. The drawings were instead converted into engravings for publication. Shown here are Waud's sketch of Wilmington between 1866 and 1871 and a final engraving of it. Drawing: Courtesy, The Historic New Orleans Collection. Engraving: Courtesy, Lower Cape Fear Historical Society*

Facing page, left: *Benjamin Franklin Hall enlisted in the Confederate Army as a young man. He was paroled at Appomattox Courthouse in 1865 and began his walk home to Wilmington. When Union soldiers offered him a ride he proudly replied, "No, we've walked this far. We'll finish on foot." Courtesy, Lower Cape Fear Historical Society*

Right: *George Davis served the Confederacy as attorney general as well as a senator from North Carolina. When he returned home to reopen his law practice it was difficult for him to get down the street without someone wanting the privilege of shaking his hand. Courtesy, Lower Cape Fear Historical Society*

toward former supporters of the Confederacy often only invoked a spirit of defiance. A song published in one of the Wilmington newspapers in November 1867 had six verses to sing out those sentiments:

And I don't want, sir, no pardon
For what I was I am;
I won't be reconstructed
If I do so may I damn.

Despite their difficulties, both blacks and whites took pride in the town's official change of status from town to city in 1866. The population stood at 18,000, and the new charter divided the city into four wards with two aldermen each. The city directory featured the new street layout with its progressive system of house numbers. Wilmington was now worthy of a chamber of commerce, which came into being the same year.

It was easier to adjust to cityhood than the new rulings coming forth from the federal government. The city was shocked to learn that General Hawley signed an order to seize the neighboring plantations of Orton, Kendall, Lilliput, and Pleasant Oaks to "set them apart for the use of freedmen and the destitute and refugee colored people." Former slaves did briefly occupy some of the land, but the decree was rescinded a few months later by President Johnson.

There was a new order of wealth in the region too. Mayor John Dawson's brother, James Dawson, had surreptitiously bought up every bale of cotton he could find, hidden it, and sold it for $300,000 in gold, which soon became part of the capital of the new Dawson Bank. Other banks had collapsed. Houses that once gleamed with fresh paint began to gray in the salt air. A new expression came into vogue: "Too poor to paint; too proud to whitewash."

New words as well as new phrases entered the Reconstruction lexicon. A "carpetbagger" may or may not have literally packed his belongings into a carpet satchel, but it was generally understood that he was an unscrupulous opportunist who left the North for the South with the objective of making money. A "galvanized Yankee" was a former Confederate soldier who enlisted in the U.S. Army—who was often destined to fight Mexicans or Indians on the Western frontier. "Scalawag" described the white Southerner in league with Republicans—many of whom were black—whose policies and use of public funds following the party's takeover of the state government in 1868 angered the majority of the populace. Wilmington had its share of carpetbaggers, scalawags, and galvanized Yankees, and the city's old-line aristocracy made it clear they had no use for any of them.

There were, however, two carpetbaggers who made profound contributions to the region's economic and educational growth. One received accolades for her efforts while the other was forced to leave town on a rail.

George Zadoc French, a bright and brash New Englander, followed the Union soldiers' wagons into town and set up shop in an abandoned building where he sold tobacco, liquor, and clothing to the soldiers, capturing the military trade. In the 1867 *Morning Star* he advertised that he had the biggest and best store in the state. When land prices fell, he bought, and his brothers joined him in a new venture, the Excelsior Plantation Company at Castle Hayne. There he discovered lime, which, combined with fertilizer, made his fields highly productive. By the early 1870s his produce was being shipped to Northern markets. His innovations with lime and truck farming

both developed into important phases of the economy. French's talents were impressive, but his politics proved unpalatable to those outside the Republican sphere; and when the Democrats regained control of the city government in 1898, "the slick-talking man" (as he was called by the *Wilmington Post*) was escorted to the depot.

Amy Morris Bradley had no interest in money or politics, but she had a mission—to educate the youngsters of Wilmington. When she arrived the odds were against her success. Outspoken, she uttered her opinions in a brusque New England twang which were offensive to the Southern ear, and her wiry frame, sharp features, and direct manner contrasted to the ideal of Southern womanhood. The fact that she was a Unitarian sent to do "good work" by the Soldiers' Memorial Society of Boston and the American Unitarian Association further alienated her from the mainstream of Wilmington society. She had intended to operate an integrated school, but upon realization that such as idea was socially unacceptable and that the American Missionary Society had already set up schools to educate 1,600 blacks, she decided to run a school for whites.

The initial parental reaction was negative; Margaret Tannahill Hall's attitude was typical of her peers: "Indeed, no child of mine shall go to a Yankee school!" Miss Bradley's school opened with only three pupils; but as Miss Bradley's reputation as a teacher grew, Mrs. Hall had a change of heart and sent her five children to Miss Bradley's, as did many others, and at the end of the term all 140 desks were occupied. In 1873 the New Hanover County Board of Commissioners unanimously voted to appoint her as the County School Examiner, the first woman in Wilmington to hold public office. The *Journal*, which had editorialized against her "evil teaching," now called her "persevering, calm tempered, and utterly fearless." Her accomplishments won her a benefactor in Mrs. Mary Tileston Hemenway, a wealthy Boston matron who donated $30,000 to her school. By 1871 a cornerstone had been laid for Tileston School. When Amy Bradley arrived in New Hanover County she found 38% of the residents illiterate; by the turn of the century the percentage had dropped to 20%.

GEORGE DAVIS
SENATOR AND ATTORNEY GENERAL OF THE CONFEDERATE STATES OF AMERICA

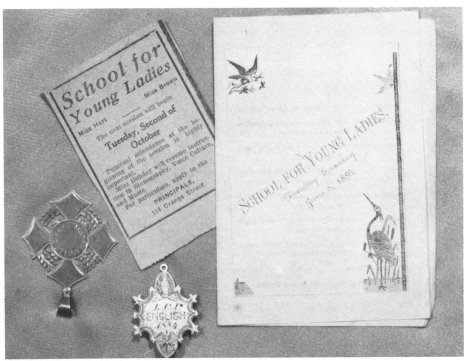

Above: *In 1866 Wilmington officially became a city, and a beehive was selected as the symbolic emblem of the city's perseverance toward industry and growth. Courtesy, Lower Cape Fear Historical Society*

Top: *Miss Kate Kennedy and Miss Annie Hart presided over one of Wilmington's most fashionable private schools for "Young Ladies." Stenography, voice culture, and music were among the courses offered. Graduation exercises were a festive affair with a recital program and the presentation of diplomas and prizes. Courtesy, Dr. and Mrs. Charles Graham*

Bottom: *Students at General Colston's Cape Fear Academy wear solemn expressions as they pose for their portrait. Prestige accompanied enrollment at Cape Fear Academy. Its curriculum emphasized the classics and the military and the school advertised that it could either "finish" a boy or prepare him for Carolina, Virginia, or a military academy. Courtesy, Lower Cape Fear Historical Society*

Emancipation provided a new status for the black community. *Smaw's 1866 City Directory* listed for the first time "A Directory of Colored Persons"—names were listed alphabetically by surname, along with street address and occupation. S.S. Ashley, Director of Free Schools, had the most prestigious title in the book. Blacks pridefully organized into special interest groups; mechanics organized the Plebean [sic] Brotherhood; and other groups, such as the Ladies Aid and Joint Stock Association, the Wilmington Rifle Guards, and a black fire department all emerged. For a time there was a Freedman's Savings Bank with John H. Smythe as cashier. Brooklyn, the black neighborhood, boasted 42 stores. By 1878 the black community welcomed the first black M.D. to practice in North Carolina—Dr. James Francis Shober. Fifty-eight percent of New Hanover County's population was, by that date, black, with a 63% electorate. This startling change in the county's electorate had come about as a result of the new federal laws. The black vote centered in the Republican party, whose local racial make-up comprised approximately 2,000 blacks and 100 to 150 whites. The white Republican faction was largely made up of the New England settlers of the 1830s and 1840s, some Germans, carpetbaggers, and a few old Whig holdouts, along with political mavericks such as Brunswick County's Daniel Lindsay Russell, who was elected governor on the Republican ticket. White leadership dominated the policy-making within the Republican party, but local blacks were elected to office, and the Reverend Henry N. Jones served as mayor pro tem in 1869.

Perhaps within the ranks of the Republican party an amicable working relationship did exist between the races, but that did not reflect the political climate of the community. Racial and political tensions ran deep; Thomas M. Cook of the *Herald* observed, "We are slumbering on a volcano." Even though the occupational forces had dwindled to 53 by 1869; and, "less than a corporal's guard of soldiers and a flock of billy and nannie goats" guarded Fort Caswell by 1874, the abuses of Reconstruction lingered. Parents instilled in their children a litany of Reconstruction horror stories. Such tales etched a lasting impression, and in an effort to escape the new social fabric the federal government tried to impose on the city, the old guard chose to ignore the new order. As the members of the white gentry busied themselves in putting their lives back in order, new social groups emerged; but the ranks of Wilmington's old-line aristocracy—though their lifestyles were less opulent than before—remained closed to outsiders, regardless of their wealth or station.

Wilmington's women rallied around the Ladies Memorial Association, whose purpose was "to rescue from oblivion the names and graves of the gallant Confederates who are buried in Oakdale cemetery." By 1868 a Confederate Memorial Day was established to fall on May 10, the anniversary of "Stonewall" Jackson's death. A visit from "The Gallant Cavalier," General Wade Hampton, who lectured on "The World's Greatest Chieftain—General Robert E. Lee," plus a visit from General Lee himself so stimulated Confederate patriotism and the fund-raising efforts of the Ladies Memorial Association that by May 10, 1872, they were able to unveil the Confederate Soldier Memorial statue at Oakdale. The day was accompanied by speeches, a Cape Fear Academy cadet drill, and music by the popular Coronet Concert Band resplendent in new grey and gold-braid uniforms.

The most exclusive club to emerge after the war was the L'Arioso German Club, which underwent slight name variations in

Top: *The Ladies' Memorial Association, whose purpose was "to rescue from oblivion the names and graves of the gallant Confederates who are buried in Oakdale Cemetery," unveiled this memorial "To The Confederate Dead" on May 10, 1872. Photo by Freda H. Wilkins*

Above: *James Edmund Willson was at one time leader of the Cornet Concert Club. When the Confederate statue was unveiled, the popular Cornet Concert Band provided the music. Cape Fear Academy cadets, also present at the event, performed a drill. Courtesy, Lower Cape Fear Historical Society*

Top: *Henry Brewington, caretaker at Wrightsville Beach, served as a North Carolina state legislator from 1874 to 1876. Though blacks were allowed to hold public office for the first time during Reconstruction, with the withdrawal of Union troops in 1876, white supremacy made a comeback. Courtesy, New Hanover County Museum*

Above: *Tournaments patterned after medieval jousts were popular in the early 1870s. Knights from the surrounding areas joined the lists to vie for the honor of selecting their favored lady to be crowned Queen of Love and Beauty. Jane Dickinson Cowan, who was selected by a knight of Virginia, reigned supreme at a ball given in her honor that evening.*

its early years. Membership in L'Arioso, a dance club, was limited to men. At first the club hosted cotillions and suppers, but in time the group also provided an opportunity for members' young female relations to make a debut. Many of these families' ladies had organized into a new group called The Ministering Circle of the National Order of King's Daughters. The Ministering Circle was a social and philanthropic group which supported many health projects to help the poor.

Most L'Arioso members also belonged to the Carolina Yacht Club, which had been formed in 1853, and which was reorganized after the war. Its first post-war regatta was a gay affair and E.E. Burruss took the cup with *Carolina*. In addition to dancing and sailing, horse racing returned after a 14-year absence. People were eager to join in the fun at the track and life seemed almost back to normal.

New institutions, as well as new buildings, made a post-war appearance. In 1871 the cornerstone for the College of Physicians and Surgeons—President, Joseph Francis King, M.D.—was laid amid much pomp and circumstance. Officers were elected to the Wilmington Public Library Association, which sponsored lectures at Masonic Hall. A popular speaker was the First Presbyterian Church's new minister, the Reverend Joseph R. Wilson. The cleric's son, Woodrow, ("Tommy") Wilson, created a local sensation with his two-wheel bicycle, thought to be Wilmington's first.

As the years went by, changes in commerce became apparent. The abolition of slavery had made rice less profitable. The naval stores industry also declined, although a bottle of turpentine remained a popular household remedy well into the new century. The 1886 discovery of phosphate, followed by marl, in the Castle Hayne area spurred the fertilizer industry. The MacRae family's Navassa Guano Company was the biggest producer, but together with its competitors—Power and Gibbs, Sans Souci, and Ace Fertilizer Companies—70,000 tons of fertilizer were produced a year. Ludwig Hansen and Andrew Smith launched the creosoting business in 1886 as founders of the Carolina Oil and Creosote Company. Peanuts from Sloop Point, Porter's Neck, and Poplar Grove plantation areas continued to provide a big export market for the North. Cotton fueled the economy, with Alexander Sprunt and Son monopolizing the compressing and export phases of the business. Donald MacRae and other businessmen launched a new enterprise with the founding of the Wilmington Cotton Mill.

The railroads continued to be an important part of Wilmington's economy, but the Cape Fear River remained the city's most important natural resource. Constant dredging and river improvements were necessary to keep the channel navigable. Between 1870 and 1882 the U.S. Congress appropriated more than a million dollars for river improvements. The most dramatic change was the damming of New Inlet. The U.S. Army Corps of Engineers included this massive project in their book of "Best Ever" achievements. Nine hundred men quarried rock near Rocky Point to provide the material to build the mighty dam known as "The Rocks." Captain Henry Bacon supervised the complex project. His son, Henry, became an architect with many fine buildings to his credit—but is most remembered for his design of the Lincoln Memorial in Washington, D.C. Not only was the river improved, but the city underwent extensive modernization throughout the 1880s. During these years the telephone, electric lights, and a public water works were all

Cotton Sampling Room, Champion Compress

Cotton Samplers.

Compressing Cotton.

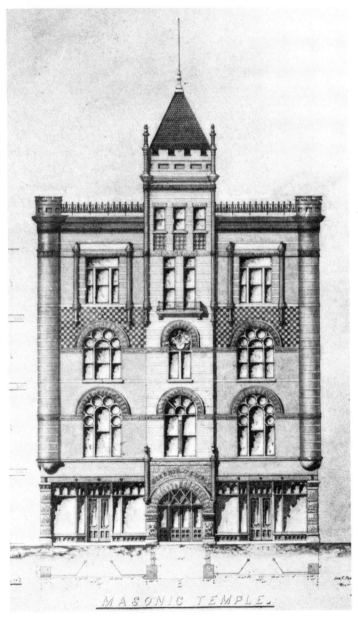

MASONIC TEMPLE.

Facing page, top: *At the Champion Compress of Alexander Sprunt and Son a huge steam-driven machine with weights took a large quantity of cotton and compressed it to one-third of its original size, producing a manageable bale that could be easily loaded on a ship. From the North Carolina Collection, UNC Library, Chapel Hill*

Bottom: *This architectural rendering of the Masonic Temple was changed radically by the time the structure was built in the 1890s. James F. Post, one of the city's busiest and most prominent architects, designed the structure. Courtesy, Lower Cape Fear Historical Society*

This page, top left: *Alexander Sprunt efficiently transformed the marketing of cotton by eliminating the middleman and providing direct steamship transportation to foreign markets. Courtesy, Lower Cape Fear Historical Society*

Top right: *Although Woodrow Wilson's biographers recall him as a sickly, studious, very serious type of youth, Wilmingtonians remember "Tommy" as a bit of a prankster. He spent the summer in Wilmington while a student at Davidson College. At that time his father, the Reverend Joseph Wilson, was pastor of the First Presbyterian Church. From the Papers of Woodrow Wilson*

Middle: *Truck farming blossomed into big business during the 1890s. Strawberries, lettuce, radishes, asparagus, peas, cabbage, and potatoes all thrived in the long growing season. By 1909 the Carolina Fruit and Truckers published their own Journal. Courtesy, Allan Strange*

Bottom: *Employees of Frank A. Thompson weigh naval stores before the barrels are loaded for shipping. Courtesy, New Hanover County Museum*

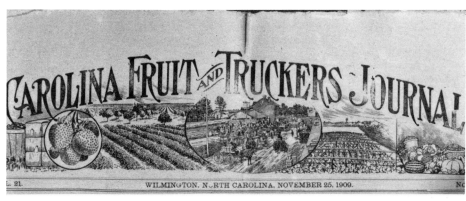

L. 21.   WILMINGTON, NORTH CAROLINA, NOVEMBER 25, 1909.   No

introduced. By 1892 John D. Bellamy's Wilmington Street Railway Company had replaced horses with electrical streetcars. A city hospital and a marine hospital had also been established.

By 1890 Wilmington's population stood at 20,000. The decade lost some of its gaiety when the First National Bank of Wilmington failed in 1891, but the community looked to the future with confidence and a cornerstone was laid for the New Hanover County Courthouse. Eventually the massive brick building with its impressive bell tower was completed; its resonant bell has tolled the city's time ever since. The Immanuel Presbyterian Church organized in 1891 and five years later one of its Sunday school teachers, Colonel Walker Taylor, organized the Boys' Brigade. A requirement for membership was Sunday School attendance—and classes filled up fast. The Church of the Good Shepard and St. Matthews Lutheran Church joined the growing number of churches.

In 1893 the Bank of New Hanover also failed, creating a panic in the business community. Colonel Kenneth McKenzie

Murchison's New York based company stepped in to save the bank and Murchison's name was soon associated with three regional landmarks: the Murchison National Bank, Orton Plantation, and the Orton Hotel.

In 1896 Wilmington society was treated to "The Kirmiss," the theatrical highlight of the year. The program, a benefit to raise funds to erect a monument to Cornelius Harnett, was billed as "a grand spectacular pageant" featuring Mrs. Andrew J. Harriss as "queen." "Spectators having weak eyes" were advised to "wear smoked glasses when witnessing . . . this . . . dazzling splendor."

Just two years later, Wilmington was to witness another spectacle—the bloody confrontation known as the Riot of 1898, which represented the culmination of political and racial grievances that had been smouldering for over 30 years. From the white point of view, the riot was a rebellion in which the white minority of 8,000 reasserted itself to recapture its position of supremacy over the 17,000 blacks. From the black point of view, it meant the end of hope for

Alexander L. Manly, editor and publisher of The Daily Record, lost his business and fled the city during the furor of the race riot of 1898. He was blamed for inciting the riot because of an inflammatory editorial he published. Careful scrutiny by scholars, however, suggests that a struggle for political power as well as racial tensions were at the root of the conflict. From the Alexander L. Manly Papers, East Carolina Manuscript Collection

By the end of the Civil War 500 Catholics lived in New Hanover County. In 1868 the Right Reverend Bishop Gibbons (pictured here in 1907) came to Wilmington as a vicar apostolic and founded a convent of the Sisters of our Lady of Mercy. While visiting Wilmington in 1876, he wrote the first chapter of Faith of Our Fathers, a simple explanation of Roman Catholicism that became a worldwide best seller. Ten years later he became a cardinal. Courtesy, Lower Cape Fear Historical Society

Fire was a constant threat in a town with so many wooden structures and homeowners who failed to keep their chimneys clean were fined. Louis Streightfellow Brown (shown here) would persuade us that he was ever ready to chop away a burning timber. Courtesy, Dr. and Mrs. Charles Graham

political and racial equality and a return to a position of impotence.

North Carolina politics compounded the problem. Republican policies were deeply resented by conservative white Democrats. The Democrats had managed to win control of the legislature in 1870, but the fusion of the newly-formed Populist party with the old Republican base increased the party's numbers enough to enable it to sweep into victory in the state legislature in 1894. The political skirmishes that erupted, as individuals and cliques grabbed for power, became ludicrous—at the height of the frenzy, four separate factions claimed victory. Elections were declared illegal; cases went in and out of court. Meanwhile, a movement was going on all over North Carolina to rid the political arena of Fusionist-Republicans. Democrats marshaled their forces on the premise that the white supremacy issue could return them to office.

William H. Bernard's *Morning Star* fanned the local racial rhetoric. Grist was provided to Bernard's mill by Alex Manley, publisher of the Wilmington black paper, *The Daily Record*, who published an editorial that defied the social taboos of his time by asserting that black women deserved as much protection from white men as white women did from black men—and he further declared that some white women seemed to enjoy the company of black men. Manley's assertions were social dynamite and the more inflammatory sections of his editorial received wide circulation and provoked near hysteria. The white community read his words as proof that their women and lives were threatened by "uppity" blacks and the white Democrats swept into office. Victory signaled a revolution and more than 1,000 people gathered to hear a new White Declaration of Independence, plus the ultimatum that a reply was to be received by a certain deadline. The black spokesmen capitulated, but added they had no real authority to speak for the black community and only wished a peaceful resolution. The courier sent by the black representatives feared entering a white neighborhood and mailed their agreement; it did not reach the white leadership before the deadline. Their presumed failure to respond was translated into refusal, and the

Colonel Kenneth Murchison saved Orton Plantation from decay following the Civil War and built a hotel in Wilmington by the same name. It was the height of elegance and home to many a traveling salesman. The Orton was destroyed by fire in 1949. Courtesy, Lower Cape Fear Historical Society

In the mid-19th century 70 percent of North Carolina's Jewish population lived in Wilmington. After the Civil War a congregation was officially organized. The Temple of Israel, the first synagogue in North Carolina, was dedicated in 1876 with Samuel Mendelsohn as its first rabbi. Courtesy, New Hanover County Museum

This page, top: *In 1910 Wilmington still led North Carolina's parade with a population of 25,748. Masted schooners still lined the wharves, and the ways of the past seemed to have returned. Courtesy, Mr. Miles C. Higgins*

Middle: *In 1909 Wilmington welcomed President William Howard Taft to the "Land of the Long Leaf Pine" with parades, banners, and a demonstration by schoolchildren dressed in red, white, and blue forming the design of the American flag. From the North Carolina Collection, UNC Library, Chapel Hill*

Bottom: *Students of the William Hooper School pose before their impressive building about 1910. It looks as though a fight is being staged at right. From the North Carolina Collection, UNC Library, Chapel Hill*

Facing page, top: *James Walker gave the City of Wilmington a gift which has never been surpassed in its magnanimity—The James Walker Memorial Hospital. The modern structure was a source of pride to the community and Solomon Bear and William and James Sprunt provided the means for additional improvements. This building was razed after the opening of the New Hanover Memorial Hospital. Courtesy, New Hanover County Museum*

Bottom: *A parade begins to form on Market Street in 1910. The lead horse was owned by Claude Howell and ridden by Colonel John Van Bokkelen Metts. Courtesy, Lower Cape Fear Historical Society*

whites banded, armed, and marched toward confrontation. Different versions of the story relate varying sequences of events, but it is agreed that the first white order of business was to destroy Alex Manley's press and burn down the building. Violence progressed from that point, and terrified black women and children raced to the woods and swamps to hide, while some black men held their ground and fought. When it was all over, three white men were wounded, 11 black men were dead, and 25 were wounded.

The old order returned in the aftermath of the riot. Democrats retained political control; the Republican party disintegrated, and its leaders, such as 70-year-old George Z. French, were given a one-way ticket North. White supremacy was reaffirmed, and the black population suffered an exodus of its most talented leaders and a 10% decline in population. As a graphic illustration of the political turnaround—the 1868 election registered 3,568 Republican votes (61.5% of the electorate), while the 1900 results tallied three Republican votes (0.1% of the electorate).

The year after the riot, a four-day snowstorm left a foot of snow on the ground, startling Wilmingtonians by the still whiteness of their city. Nature seemed determined to bring the century to a dramatic conclusion, as a November 1899 hurricane slapped the shore with fury.

Wilmington greeted the 20th century with new streets of Belgian blocks to replace the old oyster-shell streets downtown. In 1900 the first brick was being laid for the huge new hospital, which was an outright gift to the City of Wilmington from James Walker, a frugal and philanthropic bachelor who had come to Wilmington to build the Marine Hospital. Subsequent additions to the James Walker Memorial Hospital were provided by Solomon Bear, and William and James Sprunt. The next year brought Wilmington its first high school, and in 1906 the doors to the public library opened. But the library had stiff competition from the Bijou Theater, which had had its beginnings in a tent with M.W. McIntyre operating the projector that reeled out the first movie in Wilmington—"The Great Train Robbery."

With the turn of the century, the war slipped further into memory. In 1900 the U.S. government repaid St. James Church for the damages it had sustained during federal occupation. John Dillard Bellamy, Jr., who had built a house near his father's mansion where he had once watched the corpses of yellow fever victims being taken down Market Street, had been elected the U.S. Congressman from this district. And, incredibly, in 1907 old veterans staged a Blue and Gray Reunion. Former enemies met in friendship and shared a camaraderie built on the reminiscence of what all agreed had been a most significant life experience. By 1909 survivors of Fort Fisher banded in association and strenuously lobbied to have Congress make Fort Fisher a national park. That same year Wilmington hosted a tremendous reception for President William Howard Taft, who came to dedicate City Hall. School children turned out to parade, the streets were boughed in pine and draped in bunting and the Stars and Stripes flew over the city.

With a population of about 26,000 by 1910, Wilmington no longer led North Carolina's population parade, but many of the traditions of the past seemed to have returned, and masted schooners still lined the wharves of the Port City.

◆ ◆ ◆

Chapter VII
Pride and Progress from River to Sea

The Wilmington waterfront of 1912 continued to reflect its active commerce in a fast-paced drama featuring wonderful characters and memorable scenes. Captain John W. Harper, owner of the steamer, *Wilmington*, was every boy's idol. Aging Confederate veterans still spun their tales and foreign sailors still swaggered to saloons. Ships creaked against their moorings. Children fished off piers or ferried over to Eagles' Island to play on rosin barrels, as all of Wilmington followed the presidential campaign of Woodrow Wilson with parochial pride.

It was a time and place of simple delights. A penny bought a jaw-full of candy from a Greek confectionary. At the neighborhood store pickles swam in brine and hams hung in the rafters. Everyone knew the ice man, the milk man, and the hawker who sang out, "Hey . . . O! Fish, I got'em! I got butterbeans! I got corn! I got crab! I got swimps! I got 'em!" Saturday thrills hung on the serial cliffhangers at the Bijou Theater and one dreamed all year of the summer trip to the beach where sun, salt, sand, and lemonade seared the senses with halcyon memories.

The city limits ended at 10th, but at 17th and Market Miss Mary Bridger was developing the "most desirable" suburb of Carolina Heights. A suburb of more modest style had been built on the road to Wrightsville. Delgado Mills Village was a self-contained community of 700 whose fortunes depended on 15,476 spindles spinning out gingham.

There was the "good" of the good old days, but there was also the "bad," which was bred in poverty and incubated in ignorance. Wilmington had its share of run-down houses with outdoor privies, shallow wells, and unscreened windows. Such unsanitary conditions spawned typhoid fever, hookworm, and malaria. Charles Torrence Nesbitt, M.D., Wilmington's health officer, declared war on such conditions and the battle of the Establishment versus the idealistic reformer ensued. Landlords were loath to invest in improvements in property that generated little income. Nesbitt's persistence angered his foes, but in the end progress won out and the city put in a central water-sewer system as well as an incinerator. Nesbitt was not a lonely crusader; Edward Jenner Wood, M.D., son of Dr. Thomas Fanning Wood and president of the North Carolina Board of Health, made observations on sprue and pellagra that improved the quality of health in the South. In 1915 James Buren Sidbury, M.D., who practiced in Wilmington until 1967, began pioneering in pediatrics, resulting in the establishment of Babies Hospital, a pediatric hospital at Wrightsville Beach which operated until the mid-1970s.

In 1895 Mesdames Rufus W. Hicks, Andrew J. Howell, and Philander Pearsall had co-founded North Carolina Sorosis, an organization dedicated to community, cultural, and educational improvement. Sorosis campaigned vigorously for the installation of screens throughout the city. In 1915 the city got its first civic service club, Rotary International, No. 150. This altruistic organization advocated a variety of progressive improvements.

That same year, news of the German sinking of the *Lusitania* chilled the community and portended America's entry into World War I. Owen Kenan was listed as a *Lusitania* survivor, which was of interest to those who had been fascinated by his cousin Mary Lily's lavish wedding to oil magnate and Florida developer Henry Flagler — a union resulting in a fortune that endowed many community institutions.

Wilmingtonian Arthur Bluethenthal, a former Princeton All-American, was among the Americans who volunteered before the United States officially entered the war. He joined the ambulance corps, but the urge to soar skyward in the open cockpits of the new planes proved irresistible, and he donned the blue uniform of the Lafayette Escadrille, the volunteer force of Americans who joined the French in air combat. In 1918 he was killed over Coivrel, France. Fellow Wilmingtonian Harmon Chadbourne Rorison also felt the magnetic tug of aviation and became an ace pilot, who, after the war, continued his career as a member of Poland's Kosciusko Fliers. Both aviators received awards, but the most bemedaled native son was Admiral Edwin Anderson, who earned the Congressional Medal of Honor at Vera Cruz in 1914 plus two Distinguished Service Medals—one for World War I and the other for his relief work following the 1923 Tokyo earthquake.

World War I came closest to home when two German merchant ships were seized in Wilmington's harbor. The war effort intensified with the construction of George A. Fuller's Carolina Shipyard, which produced ten 1,000-ton steel freighters, while Kirby Smith's Liberty Shipyard poured concrete ships that amazed a cynical public when they proved seaworthy.

The year 1918 was a year of sorrow. Thirty-three black and 33 white men had died in World War I and 120 civilians had died from Spanish influenza. Some war dead lay buried abroad. An unusual plaque, erected by the Hanover Historical Commission at the Shrine of Bernadette in Nevers, France read: "Here lies the heart of Fr. Thomas Price." Father Price, who had been a priest in Wilmington, died in Hong Kong where he served after co-founding the Maryknoll Fathers, a Catholic foreign mission. His work fulfilled the local tradition of religious service. Adam Empie, D.D., served as West Point's first chaplain and the Reverend Augustus Foster Lyde was credited as being the founder of the Chinese Missions of the Protestant Episcopal Church. The First Presbyterian Church supported a mission in Kiang-Yin, China, a project close to the heart and pocketbook of one of the region's most beloved benefactors, Dr. James Sprunt.

By 1920 Dr. Sprunt was no longer the spritely lad who had scrambled aboard the blockade-runner, *Lilian*, but a white-haired, mustachioed gentleman whose firm handclasp, kindly heart, and lively mind offset his physical impairment of a cork leg and short stature. He and his late wife, Luola Murchison, had hospitably shared their townhouse (the Governor Dudley mansion) and their country seat

Facing page, top: *Both Thomas Fanning Wood, M.D., and his son, Edward Jenner Wood, M.D., were famous physicians of the Lower Cape Fear. Thomas Fanning Wood (left) was coeditor of the* North Carolina Medical Journal *and founder of the North Carolina Board of Health as well as being an outstanding botanist. His son Edward Jenner Wood (right) was perhaps most famous for his work on sprue and pellagra. Thomas F. Wood: Courtesy, New Hanover County Museum; Edward Jenner Wood: Courtesy, Mrs. Edward Jenner Wood*

Bottom left: *In 1891 Mary Lily Kenan, age 24, married Henry Flagler, age 61. Flagler, one of the nation's richest men—a founder of Standard Oil and developer of Florida—gave his bride a $500,000 pearl necklace and one million dollars.*

Bottom right: *Dr. James Sprunt loved the nautical heritage of the Port City and captured some of its distinctive flavor in his books. The University of North Carolina honored him with a doctorate degree for his contribution to the state's history. Courtesy, Lower Cape Fear Historical Society*

This page, top: *The steamer* Wilmington, *owned by Captain John W. Harper, made regular trips from Wilmington to Southport and Carolina Beach for the pleasure of Sunday School students and holiday picnickers. She carried 500 passengers and could reach the speed of 16 miles per hour. Courtesy, North Carolina State Archives*

Middle: *The Cape Fear Club, established in 1866, is the oldest men's club in the South in continuous existence. The club, which was originally located on the corner of Front and Chestnut streets, moved to the southeast corner of Second and Chestnut streets in 1912. This dues card dates from 1893. Courtesy, Lower Cape Fear Historical Society*

Bottom: *Beach Cars, like the one pictured here on the trestle at Bradley Creek, departed Wilmington frequently carrying excursionists to Wrightsville Beach. Courtesy, New Hanover County Museum*

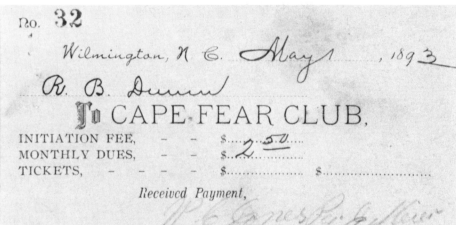

no. **32**

Wilmington, N. C. May 1 , 1893

R. B. Dunn

To CAPE FEAR CLUB,

INITIATION FEE, — — $ 2.50
MONTHLY DUES, — — $ 2
TICKETS, — — — $ $

Received Payment,

(Orton Plantation) with family, friends, and visitors. Many of those guests can still conjure up memories of the boat trip down the watery road to Orton where at the dock the American flag was dipped to each passing ship; of Mrs. Sprunt's broad pearl dog-collar necklace gleaming against her pale neck; of silver pitchers of minted iced tea, tree climbs, spooky tales of King Roger's Tomb, and the pungence of the rice fields' earth mixed with jessamine.

Dr. Sprunt turned his interest in memories into a full-time pursuit of history. He published several books, including, in 1914, *Chronicles of the Cape Fear River*, which inspired "A Pageant of the Cape Fear," a historical play that thrilled capacity audiences for four days and which was dedicated to him.

In 1924 Richard Dunlea, Sr., started broadcasting on the South's second radio station, WBBN. Listeners could have learned that native son Dr. Edwin A. Alderman, president of the University of Virginia, was delivering a memorial address on Woodrow Wilson before Congress. WBBN played music of the Jazz Age to young listeners who roared through the Twenties, largely ignoring Prohibition. The Port City was historically "wet" before North Carolina was voted "dry" by the legislature in 1909. Wilmington supported saloons galore, plus the region's biggest winery, owned and operated by Solomon Bear on Front Street. There local muscadine grapes were pressed and fermented into 200,000 gallons of wine annually.

Prohibition made such operations illegal; nonetheless, illegal distilleries, bootlegging, and smuggling became notorious big business with bullet-riddled bodies documenting their dangers. The revenue cutter, *Seminole*, snared smugglers, and her biggest triumph was the seizure of the misnamed *Messenger of Peace*, carrying a cargo of 11,916 bottles of liquor. In December 1922, crowds gathered at the foot of Market to watch revenue agents implement the court order to destroy the goods. Crates were splintered, bottles were broken, and the street was flooded in 100-proof. The repeal of Prohibition and the establishment of the A.B.C. (Alcoholic Beverage Control), with Haskell Rhett as the first chairman, created improved liquor management.

Throughout the Twenties the drinking crowd frequented the roadhouses, speakeasies, jetty parties, and private clubs, but fun could be had in a variety of ways. In 1925 George L. Nang opened the New China Restaurant, and Uncle Henry Kirkum had become famous for his oyster roasts; Lawrence Kure erected North Carolina's first fishing pier; Julius Herbst and Eugene Pickard were thrilling crowds with their speedboats, while Warren Pennington was the daredevil of the sky; Lumina, the huge wooden pavilion at Wrightsville Beach, offered music and movies over the ocean, and the new Cape Fear Hotel featured an elegant lobby. The city's new Greenfield Park, established in 1925, delighted strollers and the Kenan family had given the city a handsome fountain that splashed at Fifth and Market.

The stylish symbol of feminine liberation was bobbed hair and heightened hems; and while many local beauties followed the fashion trend, the majority of Wilmington's young women still opted for the traditional careers of marriage and homemaking. Nonetheless, a small group of trailblazers set out to prove their capabilities in a man's world.

Jane Williams MacMillan shocked her friends when, upon her husband's death in 1920, she succeeded him as a full partner in MacMillan and Cameron. She and Bruce Barclay Cameron, Sr. prof-

ited by America's infatuation with the automobile, transforming a small garage into a lucrative automotive supplies retail chain. At the same time, Lilian Baugh Rodgers earned a law degree and joined her husband as a professor at their Wilmington Law School. Annie T. Smith, M.D., joined the Bulluck Hospital staff in 1923, and in 1925 *Her* Honor, Mayor Katherine Mayo Cowan, was appointed to the office after her husband's death. But none of these professionals exhibited the free-spirited independence of Miss Elisabeth Augusta Chant, who began to exert her artistic influence upon Wilmington from the moment she checked into the Orton Hotel in 1922.

Miss Chant came to Wilmington in January, having written the Chamber of Commerce the previous year inquiring about the area's physical and artistic climate, saying that she could not tolerate another New England winter. Her studio in Levi Hart's old wine house off Cottage Lane attracted art students of varied ages, abilities, and backgrounds. Most who came under her spell were never quite the same, for Elisabeth Chant was a Bohemian and a truly gifted artist. At age 60, she glowed with vivacity, exhibiting an avant-garde approach to her life and her work that both refreshed and stimulated. She was primarily a painter but also worked in batik, which was innovative for her time.

Those outside Miss Chant's artistic sphere could see only her peculiarities and were mystified by this unconventional woman who dressed oddly, decorated her house bizarrely, and who displayed strange preoccupations with spirits and ancient primitive religions. But her students absorbed her strength, and were inspired by her originality; they developed new techniques from her demonstrations, and realized their own potential as artists. Such students as Hester Donnelly, Margaret Tannahill Hall, Claude Howell, Helen MacMillan Lane, Margaret Walthour Lippitt, Emma Lossen, Henry Jay MacMillan, Joe Nesbitt, Delbert Palmer, Irene Price, Ethel Williams, and Jane Iredell Williams felt her catalytic influence and in turn passed on her legacy to others.

Like many artists, Elisabeth Chant suffered economic hardships, but she could still feast liberally on the bounty of the region's agriculture, including a favorite local dessert, strawberries and cream. In 1926 the Chamber of Commerce boasted, "Wilmington is the center for the biggest strawberry and lettuce produce in the world and the next to the largest peanut market." Dr. Elijah Porter and the Honorable Joseph A. Brown had been pioneers in strawberry cultivation, just as others had been with lettuce. The mild climate and long growing season had made truck farming a natural industry for the region. In 1891 Daniel Webster Trask had launched a lettuce industry, which was taken up by the Hutaffs, MacRaes, and McEacherns to burgeon into a successful commercial enterprise. By the mid-1920s long lines of boxcars full of produce left the sidings of Castle Hayne, Rocky Point, and Burgaw to head north.

Hugh MacRae's innovative "business experiment in cooperative farming," which his North Carolina Development Company had promoted at the turn of the century, was in part responsible for the region's agricultural success. Agents had recruited Europeans to immigrate to southeastern North Carolina, exchanging cheap labor for 10 acres, a house, and the opportunity to live out the American dream. The surnames listed in the Burqaw, Rocky Point, and Castle Hayne telephone directories tell the story of the people who came and stayed.

Top left: *At Wrightsville Beach before the devastating fire of 1934, which burned over a hundred cottages as well as the Oceanic Hotel, a boy could boast a presentable catch of sand perch and never leave his porch. Courtesy, George Clark*

Top right: *Those who came under the influence of artist Elisabeth Augusta Chant were never quite the same. Her students absorbed her strength, were strengthened by her originality, and developed new techniques from her demonstrations. She made them realize their potential as artists whose works and lives could make a difference. Portrait by I. Henry Caliga. Courtesy, St. John's Museum of Art, Inc.*

Middle: *The Trask family was well established in truck farming by 1893, and New Hanover and Pender county fields produced vegetables and flowers that were shipped by train to the northern market. Workers are shown here harvesting gladiolus by hand about 1950. Courtesy, C. Heide Trask, Jr.*

Bottom: *Harry Edmund and Lilian Baugh Rodgers sit in rocking chairs on their porch. Lilian, daughter of a Pennsylvania governor, earned her law degree in 1918 and a year later joined her husband as an assistant professor at Wilmington Law School, which belonged to them. The school produced many well known attorneys between 1913 and 1941. Courtesy, Lower Cape Fear Historical Society*

The Dutch settled Castle Hayne. Dirk Swart typified those settlers. In Zaandam, Holland, he had tended a bridge and dreamed of owning a dairy—a dream that seemed futile. In 1912 he arrived at Ellis Island with his wife, eight children, and $107—then moved to Castle Hayne to work on a MacRae farm. By 1917 he was the proud proprietor of his own farm—the Cape Fear Dairy—and his garden and flowers supplemented the dairy income. Castle Hayne became home to many fine growers including the early families of Boet, Braak, Buis, Ludeke, Tinga, Van Bavel, Van Ness, and Verazaal.

There were a number of good reasons to come to Wilmington in the early 1900s. The City Directory stated that the city had "the handsomest Custom House in the South." New Hanover High School Wildcat fans felt sure they had the best school in the state since between 1927 and 1929 their football and basketball teams won four state titles. Mrs. Horace Pearsall had successfully organized the Wilmington Concert Association. Mr. and Mrs. William G. Robertson were devoted to this group, and arranged for one of the first concerts, featuring former St. James chorister Nelson Eddy, the operetta star who became a matinee idol.

The Great Depression of the early Thirties did not hit Wilmington as hard as it did cities whose economy was directly tied to heavy industry. Some who lived through that era recall they barely perceived a difference in lifestyle because they had always pinched pennies, stretched food, grown produce, darned socks, and enjoyed inexpensive amusements. One person allowed, "I guess we'd been poor before, but just didn't realize it." Of course economic pressures were felt—students forfeited academic plans to drop out of school to work, school books were shared, and the bicycle became a popular vehicle.

For those touched by the Depression, it was difficult to relate to the money being poured into garden improvements by Pembroke and Sarah Wharton Green Jones at Airlie. The extravagant excesses of the Joneses had fascinated Wilmington for three decades. Pembroke Jones had made a fortune in the Atlantic Coast Line Rail Road, and his wife, Sarah Wharton Green, "Miss Sadie," was wealthy in her own right. They lived in lavish style, with homes in a variety of places. At Airlie they lived in a rambling Victorian mansion and at Pembroke Park they built a beautiful lodge fashioned after an Italian villa owned by the Medicis. Those who visited Airlie told of fabulous parties where ladies won jewels for party favors, and the casual opulence dazzled even hardened socialites. At one of their parties, they delighted guests with a novel idea: they had platforms built across the huge low boughs of their gigantic live oaks, placed tables on the platforms, and served dinner aloft in the trees.

After Pembroke Jones' death in 1919, his widow married his best friend, a business associate, Henry "Harry" Walters, a large stockholder in the Atlantic Coast Line. As Mrs. Walters, she hired R.A. Toppel, a former undergardener to the German Kaiser, to transform her estate into a garden paradise. Tasteful planning and plenty of money accomplished the task, and by 1933, Airlie—with its black and white swans swimming majestically across inky lagoons—was perfect to the last detail.

Depression "Alphabet Agencies" funded municipal improvements, and Public Works Commissioner, James E.L. Wade, enthusiastically supervised the city-county program that provided a scenic drive around Greenfield Park, along with an improved drainage system. Federal funding also resulted in a new post office with a mural depicting the antebellum waterfront; and improvements at the airport, which had been built in 1927, thanks to the efforts of Addison Hewlett and other boosters.

New Hanover High School's class of 1931 didn't let the Depression dampen their spirits throughout their senior year. It would not have been difficult to predict that a class sobered by the hardships of the Depression would yield many solid citizens who made a positive difference to society, nor was it surprising that many of the college-bound became professionals and executives, while some developed their creative talents. Two boys had competed to be art editor of the annual. Ironically, Robert Ruark won out over the promising artist Claude Howell; however, Ruark deserted art for writing while a student at the University of North Carolina and went on to become a prolific novelist and nationally syndicated columnist, while Howell pursued his art studies and went on to become one of the state's most celebrated artists.

The Class of '31 lived in a community racially segregated by law and custom. Former school board chairman and U.S. District Attorney James Osborne Carr had been an early advocate of a good high school for blacks. In 1915 the Williston Industrial High School opened its doors, and in January 1931 the student body moved into the new building at Tenth and Ann.

Wilmington's black community bore the brunt of Depression hardship, but it also aspired to a better life, which was made more possible by Williston High School. The educated and economically independent black professionals paved the way to equality and the community took pride in such achievers as Frank W. Avant, M.D. and Foster F. Burnett, M.D., who provided leadership to Community Hospital and who supervised the W.P.A. improvements that resulted in the hospital's expansion in 1938.

Young blacks of the Thirties were preparing themselves for careers that would be a further source of pride to their community. Thomas Jervay was writing compositions at Williston in preparation

for his title of publisher of the *Wilmington Journal.* Herbert Bell Shaw was preparing for a life that would lead to an appointment as bishop in the African Methodist Episcopal Zion Church. Both young men might have been heartened by the news that Wilmington-born Caterina Jarboro was exciting critical audiences in Milan, Italy with her performance of Aïda in 1931. The next year she would return home to sing before a racially-mixed audience at Thalian Hall—proceeds went to the unemployed.

The unemployed were highly visible and the needs they created demanded charity that went beyond government and church programs. In the mid-1930s a group of women formed the Charity League, which metamorphosed into the Social Service League and later became the Junior League of Wilmington, Inc. This organization had been at the forefront of implementing many of the area's most innovative projects. A new airfield, named for World War I hero Arthur Bluethenthal, two Cape Fear Bridges, the community's first bookmobile, and the Wilmington Museum of Art rounded out the progress of the decade.

Wilmington coasted into the Forties and was as unprepared as the rest of the nation for the bombing of Pearl Harbor. With the entry into World War II, the community's collective heartstrings, housing, and facilities were stretched taut to meet the requirements of the war effort.

A seemingly insignificant, valueless pocosin at Holly Ridge became Camp Davis. There, the lights burned all night, and a combined civilian and military work force added $125,000 a week to the city's payroll. On one Friday afternoon so many depositors jammed the Security National Bank that an emergency exit had to be cut into the wall.

The war put Wilmington back into the shipyard business on

Left: *Surf bathing at Lumina Pavilion was only one of the offerings of the famous Wrightsville Beach pavilion. Built in 1905 by the Tidewater Power Company, the Lumina provided big name bands and a highly polished floor for dancing, organized athletic events, and at one time showed movies on a large screen erected on tall pilings at the ocean's edge. Courtesy, David Wilson*

Right: *In 1916 a new customs house was built. The old post office, the Cape Fear ferry at the foot of Market Street, the Cape Fear Club, the city hall, and the New Hanover County courthouse are prominent landmarks in this photograph. The United States Customs House, later named the Alton Lennon Federal Building, is included in the National Register of Historic Places. Courtesy, Lower Cape Fear Historical Society*

a large scale. The government appropriated $900,000 for dredging and shed construction. D.A. Orrell and U.A. Underwood supervised the North Carolina Shipbuilding Company, which soon was rolling out ships, including some christened for local heroes of the past: George Davis, Edward B. Dudley, William Hooper, Captain John Newland Maffitt, Dr. James Sprunt, Colonel Walker Taylor, and Woodrow Wilson. During the war years the population doubled and housing ran short. Civilians were urged to take in boarders—accommodations varied, from the comfort of Mrs. Devereaux Lippitt's Clarendon Plantation—where Inglis Fletcher wrote *Lusty Wind for Carolina* while her husband worked at the shipyard—to a small room at the beach. The federal government authorized the hasty construction of Maffitt Village and Lake Forest in order to house shipyard workers.

Major-General John Van Bokkelen Metts supervised the Selective Service, which sent regular "greetings" to the community's young men. Almost 7,000 went off to war. As fast as they left, new faces appeared, and the local girls found themselves being rushed by uniformed newcomers. War bulletins and wedding bells punctuated the wartime wait, and sirens signaled the blackouts.

Beach communities were warned to be alert for any suspicious activity that might indicate ship-to-shore communication. Charlotte Sprunt observed a man emerge from the Ocean Terrace Hotel and flash a light out to sea. She notified the authorities and the F.B.I. took a German spy in tow. The jeopardy of the Atlantic could be seen in the flotsam and jetsam washed ashore during the years of the U-boats. German U-boats patrolled the coastline and frequently destroyed merchant shipping. At 3 a.m. one Saturday in 1943 the alarm sirens screamed an alert. Traffic came to a standstill and darkness covered the coast. Speculative rumors as to what was happening received no confirmation. After the war it was revealed that a Nazi U-boat had surfaced off Kure Beach and fired five rounds on the Ethyl-Dow plant.

World War II pushed the population to 55,620. Rapid growth placed many demands on the city and county leadership, but mayors Bruce Barclay Cameron, Sr., and Hargrove Bellamy, as well as County Commissioner Chairman Addison Hewlett, combined their abilities to meet the challenges. Throughout the war years Rinaldo Burrus Page's newspaper, the *Wilmington Star-News*, published a regular column, the "Star News Plan," that pressed for community improvements. News of the victory was published in 1945; 148 from New Hanover County had lost their lives in World War II, but returning veterans and a postwar technology made many of the *Star*'s programs reality. Cyrus Dunlap Hogue, Sr., was an early advocate of the States Ports Authority, which the legislature approved in 1945; Mayor Cameron advocated larger riverside oil terminals, which were established. John Thomas Hoggard, M.D. campaigned for a college to accommodate returning veterans, and in 1947 Wilmington College opened its doors. The veterans also came home to find that bulldozers and DDT were turning the swamps into suburbs. As developers scrambled for deeds, the spring call of the bull alligator was replaced by the drone of the lawnmower as the suburbs stretched nearer the sea.

By the mid-1940s Greenfield Park had matured into an azalea showplace and William Houston Moore decided to build a festival around it. In 1948 the North Carolina Azalea Festival became a

Top: *T.C. Jervay, Jr., is publisher, editor, general manager and owner of the* Wilmington Journal, *one of the leading black newspapers in the South. The newspaper is located in the same building in which his father started a print shop, the R.S. Jervay Printing Company. Photo by Zalesky/Front St. Gallery. Courtesy,* Scene Magazine

Bottom: *In March of 1943 Frances Taylor prepared to launch the S.S. Walker Taylor for service in World War II. Built by the North Carolina Shipbuilding Company, the vessel was named for her grandfather, Colonel Walker Taylor, a prominent Wilmington citizen and founder of the Brigade Boys Club. Courtesy, Walker Taylor III*

reality as its president, Hugh Morton, welcomed Queen Azalea I to begin her reign. Over the years the festival developed into a popular attraction that brought thousands of visitors to Wilmington each spring. The owners of Airlie and Orton shared their gardens with festival celebrities, and people lined up to enjoy the Cape Fear Garden Club's Annual Garden Tour featuring such beautiful private gardens as Mrs. Percy Robinson Smith's in Forest Hills. In 1949 the Cape Fear Country Club hosted the First Annual Wilmington Golf Tournament and another attraction featuring nationally known participants was added to the season.

The postwar society became a society on wheels and in the summer visitors and residents alike headed to the beaches. In the late Forties and early Fifties SENCBA (Southeastern North Carolina Beach Association) promoted tourism and provided a task force to address such problems as beach erosion. However, the worst pessimist would not have predicted the devastation a hurricane named Hazel caused in October 1954. At Long Beach, 352 of the 357 buildings were eradicated. Miles of grass dunes were washed away and the beaches and sounds took a beating.

That same year the winds of social change began to howl as the U.S. Supreme Court handed down its landmark decision on school desegregation. However, local reaction to the decision's implications got lost in the shock waves of what has since been called Black Thursday—December 15, 1955—when the Atlantic Coast Line announced that within five years it would move out of Wilmington. Not since 1864 had Christmas seemed so glum. The Atlantic Coast Line was not only a part of local history, but its payroll provided sustenance for the community. In 1955 the company employed 1,500 at an annual payroll of 6.5 million dollars.

The Coast Line's departure shook the city out of lethargy, netted the city some gift property, and served as a catalyst for spectacular industrial growth. Mayor Daniel Cameron orchestrated much of the successful transition both as mayor and as one of the active participants in the formation and operation of the Committee of 100, a group that coordinated industrial recruitment.

The committee and the city proved to be super-salesmen. Corning Glass, Dupont, General Electric, and Hercules, Inc. (now Hercofina), all announced their plans to locate in the area. By 1966 Wilmington would convince the National Municipal League and Look magazine judges that it deserved the "All America City" award. Mayor Daniel Cameron gave the award presentation, which emphasized the city's successful industrial turnaround, river commerce, port development, scenic beauty and climate, and recreation, as well as its progressive outlook and other assets that added up to high livability.

The next two decades found that livability enhanced by better educational opportunities. The College of Wilmington grew into a handsome campus, and in 1968 became a university upon its acceptance into the University of North Carolina system. The Cape Fear Technical Institute was dedicated in 1967, adding a new dimension to education, while the State Marine Resources Center educated the public on the region's water resources.

A strong public school system was also an important factor in the livability quotient, and in 1969 U.S. District Court Judge Algernon Butler decreed it must be a racially integrated system. That same year the city dedicated a new bridge across the Cape Fear River, but

there was no bridge of understanding to span the gulf between the black and white communities who had lived side by side, yet cultures apart, for decades.

Television brought the violence of the Civil Rights era into Wilmington's living rooms. In those turbulent years, some local faces flashed across the screen—Williston High School graduate Joseph McNeill at a lunch counter "sit-in" in Greensboro; Hubert Eaton, Sr. M.D., filing suit after suit to implement integration in Wilmington's schools and hospitals; as well as pickets and placards, the "Wilmington 10," and angry crowds.

What viewers didn't see on television was the low-keyed approach of School Superintendent Dr. Heyward Bellamy, whose difficult task it was to placate angry white parents who did not want to integrate—while establishing a workable integration plan which would meet the court's requirements and provide an education for the children, both black and white, who were caught in the middle. Dr. Bellamy retained a cool composure while trying to convince the community that the public school system would work, despite threats, picketing, and violence.

Nor did viewers see the dedication of school board chairman Emsley Laney and John B. Cogington, M.D., or of attorney William Lanier Hill II and the school board who met whenever they had a crisis and who doggedly wrestled with plans that would best serve the students' needs, and that would be acceptable to the community, while complying with the law. Throughout the Civil Rights era, the staffs of all the schools ofen worked overtime while the student body patiently endured; and community leadership addressed each new challenge as Police Chief Elmer Williamson dedicated his force to keeping the peace.

Nonetheless, there were a number of crises reported by the media. At the apex of tension there were 35 bomb threats and 27 cases of arson, but in the end, the people who wanted integration to work persevered, and, as Dr. Bellamy summed up their dedication: "They burned the midnight oil, walked the extra mile, and in the process saved a school system."

Since that time the black community has steadily become more assimilated into the mainstream of community life. Blacks are highly visible in the marketplace. Kenneth McLaurin, E.A. "Tony" Pate, Luther Jordan, and Dorothy Johnson have all been elected to public office. Hubert A. Eaton was chosen by his colleagues to be chairman of the UNCW board of trustees and Felice Sadgwar was honored during Human Relations Week as 1982 Citizen of the Year. Thomas H. Wright III organized the St. Thomas Celebration of the Arts, which promoted an integrated effort to support a festival offering talent of both races, honoring opera singer Caterina Jarboro. The festival was a success and many regard the gala week as a community cultural and racial highwater mark.

In recent decades county voters have indicated they are willing to vote capital improvements to fund community benefits. Robert M. Fales, M.D. spearheaded the drive that culminated in the opening of the New Hanover Memorial Hospital in May 1967. County commission chairman Joseph Ward Hooper, Jr. M.D., along with Donald Brock Koonce, M.D., proudly accepted the building on behalf of the county. Voters recycled the downtown Belk-Beery Store into a modern library facility; and funds enlarged the exhibits and programs of the New Hanover County Museum. The new Law Enforcement

This page, top: *Historian Louis T. Moore poses with a bicycle like the one Woodrow "Tommy" Wilson might have ridden into the Cape Fear River. Secretary of the Chamber of Commerce for many years, Mr. Moore was tireless in his promotion of the Cape Fear area and its history. Courtesy, Mrs. William E. Perdew*

Bottom: *In 1955 the Atlantic Coast Line moved its headquarters to Jacksonville, Florida, and the buildings that housed its offices (shown here) were later demolished. Courtesy, Mr. Carl J. Oldenbuttel*

Facing page, top left: *The Atlantic Coast Line Railroad was a vital part of the local heritage with her payroll providing a living for hundreds. December 15, 1955, when the railroad announced that within five years it would move from Wilmington, became known as Black Thursday. Courtesy, New Hanover County Museum*

Top middle: *The Reverend Dr. Edward E. Kirton gave constructive input during a period of racial tension. Dr. Kirton was the rector of St. Marks Episcopal Church for over 25 years. Photo by Zalesky/ Front Street Gallery. Courtesy, Scene Magazine*

Top right: *Dr. Hubert Eaton successfully brought two suits against the New Hanover Board of Education in an attempt to improve the quality of education for Negroes. Because of his efforts all public schools in the county are required to maintain a ratio of at least one-third black children and teachers to two-thirds white students and teachers. Courtesy, Dr. Hubert Eaton*

Bottom: *This Eaton family portrait includes, from left to right, Carolyn (plaintiff in the second lawsuit), Mrs. Celeste Burnett Eaton, Dr. Eaton, standing behind him is Faustina, and young Hubert (plaintiff in first lawsuit). Courtesy, Dr. Hubert Eaton*

"25 years"
Dec. 28, 1938 to Dec. 28, 1963

Center's controversial modern silhouette casts angular shadows over Market Street.

Private organizations have succeeded in building the new St. John Gallery of Art, Inc., with its Samuel D. Hughes Gallery, along with the Cowan School of Art and the Cameron Education Center at New Hanover Hospital. The center, donated by the Cameron family, houses a library and auditorium used for continuing medical education. Cooperative efforts succeeded in building a new Girls' Club, a YWCA, and a Community Boys' Club.

Wilmington also took pride in its sons and daughters who "made good" in the 20th century: Native-born David Brinkley who began his career as a reporter on the *Star-News*; Charles Kuralt of the "On the Road" television series; Williston graduate Althea Gibson who was 1951 Wimbledon Tennis Champion; football stars Sonny Jurgensen and Roman Gabriel; boxer Sugar Ray Leonard; "Clown Prince of Basketball" Meadowlark Lemon of the Harlem Globetrotters; race car driver "Hoss" Ellington; musician Charlie Daniels; John Cheek of the Metropolitan Opera Company; and playwright Samm-Art Williams of Burgaw, whose *Home* merited a "Tony" nomination.

In a community steeped in a rich historical heritage, "progress" is often viewed as a revamping of the old to suit modern needs while maintaining the integrity of the past. Henry Jay MacMillan and Charles Hussey Boney served as chairmen to the first architectural review boards, who argued that historic buildings must be identified and salvaged in order to retain the city's distinguished architectural heritage. Almost immediately, the St. John's Art Gallery

and the Lower Cape Fear Historical Society were acting on such advice and embarking upon the restoration of two important properties to be used as their headquarters, the St. John Masonic Lodge and Zebulon Latimer House. In 1963 Mr. and Mrs. Thomas H. Wright, Jr., initiated what was to amount to a private crusade for historic preservation with their purchase of the oldest house in Wilmington, the Smith-Anderson House.

Under the Wright Chemical Company's aegis more than 30 properties were spared demolition or deterioration. Out of their method of restoration—whereby they would purchase a building and resell it to a buyer willing to restore it—the Historic Wilmington Foundation came into being. This organization specialized in restoration and handled properties as diverse as the grandiose deRosset Mansion and a string of cottages on Second. As new owners bought old houses they wanted a pedigree, and Ida Brooks Kellan and R.V. Asbury helped in the search of deeds and records to determine the history of the houses and their former occupants. By 1974 a 250-block area had been entered into the National Register of Historic Places and many a reclaimed house, with louvered frieze vents and brackets gleaming in fresh paint, displayed a Historic Wilmington Foundation Plaque to document its authenticity, while many owners proudly flew a "Residents of Old Wilmington" banner.

Native son David Brinkley urged Wilmingtonians "to develop, enjoy, and take profit" from its past, advice echoed in Thomas McCaskey's survey of the city's tourism potential in 1976. The advice was heeded and the Historic Wilmington Tour, the

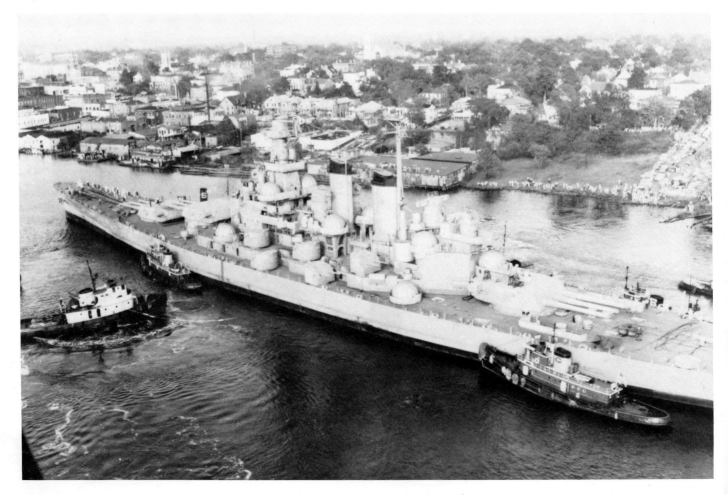

Chamber of Commerce "Cape Fear Country" Campaign, the establishment of DARE (Downtown Area Revitalization Effort), and the investment in the Cotton Exchange and Chandler's Wharf and the Water Street Plaza are all evidence of the community's commitment to revitalization. Tourism has become the region's biggest industry. A favorite spot for tourists is a bench in front of the Alton Lennon Federal Building (named for U.S. Congressman Alton Lennon) that overlooks the Cape Fear River where ducks cavort in the wake of red tugboats, and the mighty battleship, USS *North Carolina*, stands vigilant over the harbor.

Tourists are also attracted to the hustle and bustle of shopping at Independence Mall, the serenity found at Orton, Airlie, and Greenfield Park, the restored Poplar Grove Plantation, and the drama of the Blockade Runners of the Confederacy Museum. This is a spot where sportsmen are challenged by the marlin in the spring and the blue fish in the fall. The sky is the Atlantic Flyway and its Carolina blue is punctuated by the silhouettes of birds and the eerie "ticktack" patterns of white jet fantails. Sand castles, condominiums, and gray-shingled cottages share the white strand, and colorful sails dot the sounds.

The Cape Fear is a region of natural beauty and those who stay long enough see the sounds and marshes dappled by the changing seasons. Tourists must share this place with more than 100,000 people who call it home and who count their days by a sun that rises out of the Atlantic and sets past the Cape Fear River.

More than 100,000 sunrises ago, Captain William Hilton sailed the *Adventure* up that river in quest of a discovery of a new land ripe for settlement. He came in the bright blue weather of October when the air was crisp and the pines shimmered in the sun. Hilton sounded the waters and scouted the sandy bluffs and delighted in the natural bounty of his discovery. Generation after generation after generation have shared Hilton's view, and so the Cape Fear adventure goes on.

> "But the majestic River floated on,
> Out of the mist and hum of that low land . . ."
> —Matthew Arnold

◆ ◆ ◆

Above left: *Native son and newscaster David Brinkley encouraged Wilmingtonians "to develop, enjoy, and take profit" from their city's past. Brinkley attended New Hanover High School and worked for a time at the Wilmington Star-News. Courtesy, David Brinkley*

Above right: *Fishing off the Cape Fear is as old as time. George Clark probably knew more about fishing, fished more, and caught more fish than any other sport fisherman in the area. He was a frequent sight along the beaches and usually had a handsome catch of sheepshead, drum, and weakfish when others were unable to tempt a bite. Here he displays a delicious pair of weakfish. Courtesy, George T. Clark, Jr.*

Right: *In 1966 Wilmington won the "All America City" award. Daniel Cameron gave the winning presentation which emphasized the city's livability. Courtesy, Star News Newspapers*

Left: *The only American battleship to take part in all 12 major offensive naval campaigns in the Pacific during World War II was the U.S.S. North Carolina. Now berthed at Wilmington, the "Immortal Showboat" serves as a memorial to all of North Carolina's war dead and attracts visitors from all over the nation. Courtesy, East Carolina Manuscript Collection*

The centennial shield of the City of Wilmington incorporates many elements: the city, the river, the naval stores industry (top corners), Spencer Compton, the Earl of Wilmington (bottom left corner), the University of North Carolina, most probably George Washington (bottom right corner), and the North Carolina State seal (bottom). Courtesy, John Robert Lane, Jr.

Zebulon Latimer built this elegant Italianate house on South Third Street in 1852. The Lower Cape Fear Historical Society purchased the house from the Latimer family in 1963 and has restored it as a house museum and as its headquarters.

LATIMER
HOUSE
1852

LOWER CAPE FEAR
HISTORICAL SOCIETY
INC.
HEADQUARTERS

OPEN
TUESDAY-SATURDAY
10:00 A.M.-5:00 P.M.

An 1865 view of Wilmington depicts released
prisoners on their way to transport ships. Also
shown are blockade runners, David D.
Porter's fleet, the custom house, the Cape Fear
River, the town hall, and various churches
and residences. Courtesy, Dr. and Mrs.
Lucien S. Wilkins

Above: The Pride of Baltimore brought back memories of the ships which once lined the harbor of the Port City. The clipper helped celebrate the completion of Waterfront Park in 1982.
Right: Coastal Carolina counts its days by a sun that comes out of the Atlantic off Wrightsville Beach.

A tugboat moored at the Stone Towing Line dock waits to nudge a ship upriver and under the bridge to a safe berth in Wilmington.

Spinnakers fill with wind as ocean racers compete off Wrightsville Beach.

Once again the brown pelican has become a familiar sight on coastal pilings. A new, thriving rookery on a Cape Fear River island insures that their young will get a head start on survival.

Left and Facing page: *Nature blessed the Lower Cape Fear with botanical splendors that have delighted observers for centuries: Indians brewed the Yaupon's leaves (left) into a purgative tea, daffodils (facing page, top) butter the old bulb fields at Rocky Point and Castle Hayne, irises at Orton (bottom left) reflect a serenity of dark pools, and 10 million azaleas (bottom right) are worthy of celebration in an annual spring festival.*

Below left: *Johnny Mercer's Pier, a Wrightsville Beach landmark, is silhouetted on the sand by a sun rising from a glassy Atlantic. During the fishing season anglers crowd the rails at Johnny Mercer's hoping to entice flounder, bluefish, or even spot to take a bait.*

Facing page: *Orton Plantation, overlooking lovely gardens, old rice fields, and the Cape Fear River, was built in 1735 by "King" Roger Moore. In the 19th century Orton was among the leading rice producers in the Lower Cape Fear. In the early part of the 20th century the Murchison and Sprunt families added wings to the house and developed the extensive gardens.*

This page, top and middle: *Orton Plantation symbolizes the best of antebellum southern tradition in hospitality and grandeur. The gardens attract visitors year round.*
Above and bottom: *Mrs. Pembroke Jones, later Mrs. Henry Walters, took a beautiful spot and transformed it into Airlie Gardens, which has been described as "Earth's paradise in all its glory."*

Left: *Wilmington takes special pride in its municipal park at Greenfield Lake. Its azalea-lined shores make a spectacular spring show and a quiet beauty is also evident in autumn.*

Top: *The Lower Cape Fear Historical Society annually sponsors "Old Wilmington by Candlelight." For this tour the historic district glows with soft light and is decorated for the Christmas season—a combination that draws visitors from all over North Carolina.*

Above: *The National Cemetery was established to accommodate the Union dead after the fall of Wilmington in 1865. It is now the final resting place for veterans of many wars and reflects a peaceful serenity.*

Above: *Armand J. deRosset III, M.D., a third generation Wilmington physician, built this Italianate mansion in 1842. It is now owned by the Historic Wilmington Foundation, Inc. which plans to restore it to its former glory.*

This page, top: *The Burgwin-Wright House was built by merchant John Burgwin about 1770 on the foundations of an abandoned jail. During the Revolution the British used the jail as a dungeon, and local tradition has it that Cornwallis commandeered the house as headquarters before marching on to Yorktown and surrender. The National Society of Colonial Dames of America in the State of North Carolina purchased the property and has carefully restored the house and 18-century gardens.*

Bottom: *The Dudley Mansion is headquarters for the Historic Wilmington Foundation which is dedicated to the preservation of sites and buildings of historical and architectural significance. The house was built by Governor Dudley and later occupied by Pembroke Jones, financier, and by Dr. James Sprunt, historian and philanthropist.*

Facing page: *The Bellamy Mansion has dominated the corner of Fifth and Market streets for over a hundred years. It was built in 1859 for Dr. John Bellamy, physician, rice planter, and board member of the Bank of Cape Fear and the Wilmington Weldon Railroad.*

This page, top: *The classic Greek portico graces the facade of the Cape Fear Club, the oldest men's club in continuous operation in North Carolina.*

Middle and bottom: *In the 1840s vents and brackets became a familiar architectural detail of Wilmington's Italianate houses. The ornate brackets support heavy eaves and the vents permit circulation of air in the attic. These vents and brackets are on the Zebulon Latimer House (middle) and the deRosset House (bottom).*

Facing page, top left: *The afternoon sun transforms the stained glass of a First Presbyterian Church window into jewels of sapphire and ruby. This gothic church, occupied by Wilmington's First Presbyterian congregation, was begun in 1927 and stands on the northeast corner of Third and Orange streets.*

Top right: *In 1729 St. James Parish was founded by an act of the Colonial Legislature, and as such, is the oldest church in Wilmington in continuous use. The cornerstone of the first church was laid in 1751. During the Revolution it was seized by British troops under Cornwallis and converted into stables and a riding school for Tarleton's dragoons. During the Union occupation of Wilmington the present church was seized and used as a hospital for Union wounded.*

Bottom left: *The graceful curve of this porch stair suggests hospitality and invites one within.*

Bottom right: *Sanwood carpenter's lace embellishes the bargeboard and frieze of this 1880s house.*

*Wilmington is North Carolina's
most important port. The Cape
Fear River provides sustenance to
the community, attracts businesses,
and stimulates commerce.*

Chapter VIII

Partners in Progress

by James Robert Warren

In 1526 de Ayllon's construction of a Spanish ship at the mouth of the mighty Cape Fear River set the stage for an intriguing economic drama that has spanned four and one-half centuries. Two years earlier Verrazano had described to the King of France "the open Countrey rising in height above the sandie shoare with many faire fields and plaines, full of mightie great woods, some very thicke, and some thinne, replenished with divers sorts of trees, as pleasant and delectable to behold, as is possible to imagine." This explorer's account and the scenes of history that were to be enacted laid the foundation for tourism, ultimately the area's chief industry.

Wilmington, now the major port of North Carolina, is situated on the east bank of the Cape Fear River at its convergence with the Northeast River. This protected colonial port provided the center for transportation of goods to and from the plantation system and the largest exportation of naval stores in the British Empire. Tales of pirates' rendezvous and Indians stalking through moss-draped forests preceded the strife of the American Revolution. The clash of the War Between the States, when Wilmington was chief cotton port and the last open port of the Confederacy, and the imperious Reconstruction played havoc on the moonlight-and-magnolia glamour of a prosperous antebellum scene. That southern spirit of manhood, both white and black, conquered the ensuing problems to live in harmony as a new South emerged. The Great Depression brought tribulations, but the people had their ingenuity and land on which to depend. World wars created a thriving shipbuilding industry. The Atlantic Coast Line, whose progenitor the Wilmington &

Weldon was once the longest in the world, remained headquartered in Wilmington until mid-20th century. The link between rail and sea continued to provide a transportation focal point for industries such as fertilizer manufacture, truck farming, commercial fishing, and lumber as new enterprises were attracted. The stage was being set for yet a new era.

A new virtuoso sallied forth. A new vibrant Wilmington emerged with its focal point on tourism built on tradition and heritage. The supporting actors for this scenario are the diversified economic units of Cape Fear Country. The formation of the Committee of 100 and the continuing efforts of the Greater Wilmington Chamber of Commerce, North Carolina's oldest, are attracting new industries as older enterprises modernize and expand. A major university, expanded educational opportunities, and a rich cultural heritage provide impetus for an awakening spirit. As rediscovery of a superb architectural heritage has stimulated preservation of the old central business district and the Historic District, the city and the region expand, offering a regional shopping mall, air transportation, and the fastest growing state ports authority on the East Coast. Beautiful beaches, water sports, golf, tennis—all complement the many historical attractions related to the history of the mighty Cape Fear River.

The new Wilmington, once North Carolina's largest city, realizes its important place in time and is preserving it as one of America's most historic and beautiful cities—a salute to a diversified economy as portrayed in the following pages.

ATC Petroleum, Inc.

ATC Petroleum, Inc., is often referred to as ATC Energy, because of its versatility as an energy producing company. This Wilmington crude oil processing refinery is the only one located in the state. Incorporated in its refinery design is a high degree of flexibility and efficiency. Constructed in 1971, the plant at 801 Surry Street is completely staffed to ensure its compliance with all local, state, and federal environmental regulations.

With a rated capacity of 500,000 gallons a day or 182.5 million gallons annually, the facility was originally designed to produce automotive gasoline. In order to meet the needs of an increasingly diversified roster of customers, however, the plant was adapted in 1976 to produce heating oil and heavy fuels also, especially the numbers four, five, and six grades used in various industrial plants.

Distribution of products from the facility to customers is normally by a fleet of 150 independent tank trucks, a veritable "pipeline-on-wheels." However, barge deliveries of fuel oil via the Inland Waterway are also used for large-volume customers as well as deliveries by railcar.

ATC is supplied with petroleum products under long-term contracts with the Venezuelan government. It also obtains products from Gulf and West Coast refineries. Three modern tankers, acquired by the Axel Johnson Group, with a total capacity of 130,000 deadweight tons, are under contract to ensure a constant supply of fuel oils from offshore United States. These ships are regularly checked to ascertain that they meet the strictest environmental standards.

ATC Energy is a part of A. Johnson & Co., Inc., New York, which is involved in a wide range of activities throughout the United States. Other subsidiaries of A. Johnson & Co., Inc., include Ingersoll Johnson Steel Company located in New Castle, Indiana, which is the only fully integrated specialty steel mill in the Midwest; Bird-Johnson Company of Walpole, Massachusetts, which supplies controllable-pitch propellers to the marine industry and the U.S. Navy; Parkson Corporation, located in Fort Lauderdale, Florida, which manufactures water and wastewater treatment equipment; C.H. Sprague & Son Company, based in New Hampshire, which is one of the largest fuel oil distributors in the Northeast; A. Johnson Petroleum Company, based in Houston, Texas, which carries out supply and trading activities related to crude oil and finished petroleum products; and Axel Johnson Exploration and Production Corporation, located in Houston, Texas, which explores and develops oil and gas properties. A. Johnson & Co., Inc., is also involved in the manufacture and sale of stainless steel and steel products, as well as shipping.

With a quality line of products, outstanding service, security of supplies, and the most modern laboratory facilities in North Carolina to ensure excellent quality control, ATC Energy has good reason to think of itself as "the energy company." ◆ ◆ ◆

ATC Petroleum, Inc., the only crude oil processing refinery in North Carolina, is located at 801 Surry Street, Wilmington.

Atlantic Telecasting Corporation

across the Cape Fear River. A 1,000-foot tower was constructed at Delco in 1956. Then, in 1968, a dramatic event in the company's history occurred when it moved its antennae to White Lake. The coverage area was tremendously increased with the construction and use of this new 2,000-foot tower. For many years this was the highest man-made structure east of the Mississippi River. With this new addition, WECT became a regional rather than a local broadcasting corporation.

On October 15, 1954, Hurricane Hazel devastated the Cape Fear coastal areas, and Channel 6 gave viewers the first comprehensive coverage of the local disaster. Another example of WECT's community involvement and fine coverage was the arrival of the U.S.S. *North Carolina* in the Wilmington harbor in October 1961. This was a dream originated by WECT executive Jimmy Craig. Channel 6 had statewide telecast of the arrival and the dedication. Atlantic Telecasting Corporation strives to keep the region informed. It now telecasts over 18 hours a day, including three hours of local news every weekday. The weekly viewing audience has grown from a few thousand persons to over 600,000 people. Viewpoints from all walks of life are sought and expressed. The company continues its strong policy of supporting local institutions and events. As an NBC affiliate, it maintains quality media for Wilmington and southeastern North Carolina.

◆ ◆ ◆

WECT-TV, Channel 6, strives to keep Wilmington and the surrounding area informed, aided by on-the-spot coverage of local events.

Located at 322 Shipyard Boulevard, WECT-TV now telecasts over 18 hours a day, including three hours of local news.

◆ ◆ ◆

became Atlantic Telecasting Corporation. The corporation expanded its interests by buying Pepsi-Cola franchises. Pepsi-Cola became a larger part of the enterprise than the television station, and in 1972 Atlantic Telecasting Corporation became a subsidiary of Atlantic Pepsi, a publicly held corporation with 600 stockholders. The Pepsi-Cola operations were sold in 1979, and Atlantic Telecasting Corporation reverted back to being a single-station public corporation. Dan Cameron is president and chief executive officer; J.S. Brody is chairman of the board; C.D. Martin, Jr., is executive vice-president and general manager; and Bruce Cameron is secretary-treasurer.

The firm's first location was on Princess Street between Second and Third streets. Studio facilities and offices were constructed at 322 Shipyard Boulevard in 1959. The first tower was the WMFD-Radio tower located just

WMFD-TV, Inc., was founded in 1954 by R.A. Dunlea and MacMillan and Cameron Company. With the advent of television and the availability of Channel 6 to Wilmington, North Carolina, WMFD-TV was the only applicant to the Federal Communication Commission for the frequency. Thus, television first aired in Wilmington on April 9, 1954, with a five-hour-a-day telecast from 6 p.m. to 11 p.m. On February 18, 1955, Channel 6 interconnected with NBC and brought live network programs to the viewing audience. When Atlantic Telecasting Corporation replaced WMFD-TV, Inc., WECT came into effect on February 15, 1958.

R.A. Dunlea served as the first chairman of the board, and R.A. Dunlea, Jr., was the first president of the corporation. Dan Cameron became president and chief executive officer in 1957. While MacMillan and Cameron Company maintained its stock, the Dunleas sold their interest to J.S. and Leo Brody, J.W. Jackson, and the WNCT television station of Greenville. At this time WMFD-TV, Inc.,

Bland & Associates, REALTORS, Better Homes and Gardens

Bland & Associates, REALTORS, Better Homes and Gardens, located at 4110 Shipyard Boulevard, Wilmington.

◆ ◆ ◆

Elizabeth W. Bland strongly believes in the work ethic. She values free enterprise and believes that if you plan to do something, you should plan to do it right. This dynamic woman has been a licensed REALTOR for 13 years, rapidly becoming noted in the real estate field. This coincides with her philosophy of continuing to improve one's self and successfully accomplishing all that one attempts.

Mrs. Bland has owned her own business for nine years. In August 1979 she, as sole owner, opened Bland & Associates, REALTORS, Better Homes and Gardens. In October 1981 she moved to her new 4110 Shipyard Boulevard office building, constructed and landscaped according to her design of aesthetically blending architecture with the environment. Bland & Associates, REALTORS, Better Homes and Gardens has an all-woman staff, including 15 independent contractors.

Mrs. Bland is a University of North Carolina at Chapel Hill graduate of REALTORS Institute (GRI). She is a certified resi-

dential specialist (CRS), achieved by completing required courses and marketing a certain number of residential properties in a professional manner. At the University of North Carolina-Chapel Hill she completed Courses 1A and 8 as prerequisites toward the residential appraisal designation. Real estate law studies were taken at the University of North Carolina at Wilmington.

Mrs. Bland feels that the constantly changing financial market requires expertise and continuing education about financial trends. Everyone associated with her firm is a full-time professional broker, six having completed the GRI designation. She maintains an awards program rewarding her sales associates.

Better Homes and Gardens Real Estate Service is an affiliation consisting of 2,200 offices throughout the United States. The firm

is a subsidiary of the Better Homes and Gardens publishing service. The real estate service handles referrals nationwide, and Mrs. Bland was chosen as an affiliate based on her professional image in the community. Bland & Associates, REALTORS, Better Homes and Gardens is a full-service organization that works closely with the local industry relocation process. Eighty percent of the firm's sales deal with relocation. Extensive training of associates provides special services to help new residents become integrated into the community.

Mrs. Bland has been recognized as the 1981 REALTOR of the Year by the Wilmington Board of REALTORS. This distinctive honor was bestowed on her by a committee of past winners for her integrity, professionalism, and contributions to the community. She has served as treasurer, program chairman, multiple listing chairman, and director for three terms of the Wilmington Board of REALTORS. As Make America Better chairman, her committee won the state's second place award for providing a Wilmington historical excursion for foster children. Mrs. Bland is past Woman of the Year of the U.S.S.N.C. Business Women's Association. She serves as chairman of the New Hanover County Soil and Water Conservation District Board of Supervisors. As a member of Executives Club, Committee of 100, Chamber of Commerce Political Affairs Task Force, New Hanover Home Builders, and a mother of four, Elizabeth Bland serves home and community with dynamic enthusiasm.

Bland & Associates, REALTORS, Better Homes and Gardens is a proud example of what dedication and professionalism can produce in our free enterprise system. Mrs. Bland's accomplishments have proven that her philosophy does, indeed, work.

◆ ◆ ◆

Elizabeth W. Bland, GRI-CRS, owner of Bland & Associates, REALTORS, Better Homes and Gardens.

Carolina Bottlers, Inc.

Carolina Bottlers, Inc., is a holding company for the purpose of consolidating three individual soft drink bottling and distributing corporations that had been based in Wilmington since the 1930s. The three firms that operated separately and autonomously were Pepsi-Cola Bottling Corporation of Wilmington, Seven-Up Bottling Company of Wilmington, Inc., and Dr Pepper Bottling Company of Wilmington. The entrepreneurial spirit of Donald R. Watson and Carl B. Brown, Jr., is responsible for the establishment of the current enterprise, which manufactures and distributes Pepsi-Cola, Diet Pepsi, Mountain Dew, Dr Pepper, Sugar Free Dr Pepper, Seven-Up, Diet Seven-Up, Sunkist, Nugrape, and Brownie Chocolate.

The three major soft drinks have a fascinating history. The creator of Pepsi-Cola was Caleb D. Bradham, a North Carolinian born in Chinquapin. As a young pharmacist and owner and operator of a drugstore in New Bern, North Carolina, Bradham started concocting soft drinks for his friends. With experimentation he developed a new beverage and started offering it at his soda fountain in the 1890s. His cronies hailed it as excellent and called it "Brad's Drink." By August 28, 1898, Bradham had given it the name Pepsi-Cola. Eventually, radio's first singing commercial was to advertise his discovery. Noted chemist C.L. Grigg origi-

nated Seven-Up in St. Louis, Missouri, in the 1930s. A story of the origin of the name is that while on a train ride through Texas, Grigg saw a cow branded "7 U," and this unique feature inspired the name Seven-Up. Dr Pepper was created in 1885 in the bustling pioneer town of Waco, Texas, by Dr. Charles C. Alderton. Dr. W.B. Morrison, proprietor of The Old Corner Drugstore of Waco, collaborated with his pharmacist employee Dr. Alderton in developing the Dr Pepper formula. Dr. Morrison gave Dr Pepper its name—to favor a Dr. Pepper, who had discouraged an early budding romance with his daughter.

Dr Pepper and Pepsi-Cola were distributed in Wilmington by J.W. Jackson in the early 1930s. He relinquished Dr Pepper when he received the Pepsi-Cola franchise and formed Pepsi-Cola Bottling Company of Wilmington. In 1963 it was sold to Atlantic Telecasting Corporation. A group, organized by Donald R. Watson and S. Douglas Fleet of Richmond, Virginia, purchased Pepsi-Cola Bottling Corporation of Wilmington in 1965.

In 1935 Lloyd Brown, a bottler in Durham, told his brother Carl B. Brown, Sr., that he was offering a new product, Seven-Up. Carl B. Brown, Sr., bought a Seven-Up truck and began developing distribution, eventually reaching Wilmington. Carl Brown, Sr., moved with his wife Minnie, his daughter Jean, and his

son Carl B. Brown, Jr., to Wilmington. In association with his brother Lloyd, in 1938 he established the Seven-Up Bottling Company of Wilmington, Inc., at 17th and Castle streets for the distribution of Seven-Up bottled in Raleigh. In 1949 bottling equipment was acquired and Seven-Up was bottled for the first time in Wilmington under the direction of Carl B. Brown, Sr., at the 1946 relocation at 17th and Dawson streets.

In 1967 the franchise to bottle Dr Pepper, which was then distributed in Wilmington by Roberson's Beverages, Inc., of Washington, North Carolina, was acquired by a newly formed Dr Pepper Bottling Company of Wilmington, organized by Watson and Fleet.

Two years later Carl B. Brown, Jr., Watson, and Fleet acquired the equity of Carl B. Brown, Sr., Lillian Brown, and the estate of Lloyd Brown, in Seven-Up Bottling Company of Wilmington, Inc.

Fleet tendered his stock in each of the corporations for redemption in 1976. Entrepreneurs Watson and Brown founded Carolina Bottlers, Inc., and completed the consolidation of the three local companies. Watson serves as president and Brown is executive vice-president.

◆ ◆ ◆

This is the headquarters of Carolina Bottlers, Inc., located in Wilmington.

Carolina Power & Light Company

March 1, 1886, marked the dawn of electric service in Wilmington, but there was strong opposition from residents who claimed that the intense lights drew water bugs from the river in numbers menacing to the public health.

Wilmington's first lights were arc lights, strung on sections of Front and Market streets as well as at downtown businesses such as the Orton Hotel. The city contracted for similar light service that began on July 1, 1886, only four years after Edison began his commercial generation of electricity in New York City. Wilmington Electric Lighting Company supplied the power.

Electric lights were soon followed by electric streetcars and a steam-powered train that ran to Wrightsville Beach. Wilmington's street railway, its railroad to the beach, and the gas company (which had taken over the electric lighting company) merged on April 23, 1902, to form Consolidated Railways, Light and Power Company. Consolidated installed the first steam turbine generator south of the Mason-Dixon line.

To finance a tremendous expansion of the utilities, Tide Water Power Company was organized on February 27, 1907, and leased the properties of Consolidated. During the Depression years, control of Tide Water Power Company changed hands many times. In 1952 it was merged into Carolina Power & Light Company. The takeover of Tide Water represented the last major geographical expansion for CP&L, a company that serves northeastern South Carolina, eastern North Carolina, and the Asheville area in western North Carolina.

Shortly after CP&L began serving the Wilmington area, the company started construction of the Louis V. Sutton Plant. The first unit was completed in 1954, followed by the addition of five other units for a total generating capacity of 652 megawatts. The new plant exemplified the expansion of existing industry in Wilmington and was instrumental in attracting new industry. More than 160 industries announced plans to build or expand. Demand for electricity had increased sixfold since the 1952 merger, and in 1970 CP&L began building another generating plant.

Construction of the Brunswick Steam Electric Plant took seven years and represents an investment of $714 million. Located just north of Southport, the plant has two boiling-water nuclear reactors with a generating capacity of 1,580 megawatts. When unit one began operation in November 1975, it was North Carolina's first nuclear power generating unit.

The Brunswick and Sutton plants are evidence of CP&L's commitment to the growth of Wilmington. The firm serves more than 80,000 customers and employs over 600 residents in the Wilmington district.

Carolina Power & Light Company is dedicated to providing reliable electric service. CP&L's plans in the '80s call for continued reliance on coal and nuclear power for its electrical generation, while diligently promoting load management and energy conservation.

Construction of the Louis V. Sutton Plant, situated on the Cape Fear River north of Wilmington, began in 1952. Today the plant has three coal-fired units and three oil-fired internal-combustion turbines.

Cherry, Bekaert & Holland

The story of Cherry, Bekaert & Holland, Certified Public Accountants, began on August 16, 1947, when Harry W. Cherry, CPA, opened his office at Seven Trust Building in Wilmington, North Carolina. After graduating from the University of North Carolina at Chapel Hill with a degree in accounting, he first developed a sound foundation in his profession. With a desire to apply the skills he had learned to his own office, he ventured out on his own as an individual practitioner with one employee. From these modest beginnings, the firm has seen a spiral of growth to 24 offices in six southeastern states, employing over 400 people. It is rated as one of the 20 largest CPA firms in the United States. The key to its growth has been the ability to offer the resources of a large firm, yet retain the local identity and personalized client relationships.

Charles J. Bekaert, a University of Kansas alumnus, joined the firm in 1950. The name became Cherry and Bekaert in 1952. That year William S. Holland, an outstanding student at the University of North Carolina at Chapel Hill, joined the business. Two years later, in 1954, Holland became a partner and the firm took its present name of Cherry, Bekaert & Holland. Their individual talents blended together to form a most successful team.

Through the years, a strong management base for the future of the organization was built. Although the original three partners have retired, the influence of Wilmington continued with the election of Gary J. Wolfe, a Wilmington native, as the firm's managing partner in 1978.

◆ ◆ ◆

Today's Wilmington partners are (left to right) David G. Whaley, William L. Lanier, Jr., and L. Eddie Dutton.

The three original partners believed strongly in keeping their minds open to new ideas, observing the highest professional standards and always providing opportunities for other talented individuals. Quality service to its diversified list of clients created a solid base for growth which has accelerated over the years.

The first branch office was established at Myrtle Beach, South Carolina, in 1956. In succession, offices opened throughout the southeastern United States. Cherry, Bekaert & Holland expanded its abilities when it bought its first computer in 1965, and now the computer center serves both the firm's clients and those of over 350 other accounting firms in the country. With growth, an impressive array of talents has been assembled. Some of the finest tax minds in the country are represented in the organization. The management services department provides

The original partners of the firm were (left to right) Charles J. Bekaert, Harry W. Cherry, and William S. Holland.

◆ ◆ ◆

consulting services to management of clients on a variety of subjects. The firm is represented at the national level on the Auditing Standards Board of the American Institute of Certified Public Accountants. Professional staff members are kept current on professional matters through continuing education provided by the in-house education department.

Through its unique combination of being able to provide all the advantages that size affords but still retaining personal service to clients, Cherry, Bekaert & Holland will no doubt be a significant force in the future world of professional accounting.

D. & L. Trucking Inc.

L.M. Roach founded D. & L. Trucking Inc. based on a philosophy of service to the client. He feels that the customer is number one and expects to be treated as such, receiving the utmost in quality service. The company concept was originated by Roach in 1972 while he was working as a United States government employee at Sunny Point Terminal south of Wilmington. He realized the need for additional trucking service to handle the loading and unloading of ships docking at Sunny Point Terminal and the Port of Wilmington. Initially, the business operated on a part-time basis dealing with the importation of fish meal from Peru. When the trucks were not being used to service the fish meal ships that arrived every 90 days, Roach used them to aid in delivery of materials for the construction of Disney World in Florida.

As the Russians started to corner the world market on fish meal and the United States domestic market ceased to purchase the item from the Peruvian government, Roach decided that it was time to venture out and become a full-fledged trucking company. D. & L. Trucking is primarily a contracting organization. Cargo is unloaded and moved to the receiving plants. Service can then be provided to move the material from the plants to points of destination. The firm's initial contract was with Almont Shipping Company. Cargill, Inc., W.R. Grace & Co., Linden Chemical Company, Ideal Basic Industries,Inc., and Northeast Chemical Company are organizations for which D. & L. Trucking Inc. provides service as it rapidly expands. It has the contract with the state of North Carolina to cover the state with ice and snow salt. It also maintains the salt level for Mt. Olive Pickle Company at Mt. Olive, and Cates Pickle Company at Faison.

Available cargo-handling equipment has grown from 15 to approximately 75 pieces. The company has expanded from an 8-foot by 20-foot office and garage to a 6-acre industrial development park on Highway 421 with a 60-foot by 60-foot shop and a 20-foot by 40-foot office building. Employees have increased from 3 to 35. A double-shift maintenance department is retained. The company's operations encompass pneumatic tanks, liquid tanks, open hydraulic dumps, flatbed trailers, and lowboy trailers. Primary hauling is in North Carolina, but service is provided to much of the East Coast. W.R. Grace & Co., Diamond Shamrock Corporation, and others are supplied with raw materials on a daily basis. Their products are then transported to the various shipping points.

D. & L. Trucking Inc.'s rapid success has been a result of L.M. Roach's energetic enthusiasm. He offers quality and versatility in his service, and his clients are quick to realize that this is Wilmington's prime trucking company.

◆ ◆ ◆

D. & L. Trucking Inc. taking part in the 1982 Azalea Festival.

Dorothy's Ruffled Originals, Inc.

Dorothy Noe, owner of Dorothy's Ruffled Originals, Inc.

D orothy's Ruffled Originals, Inc., based in Wilmington, is a prime example of what can happen under the American free enterprise system. One woman with initiative, perseverance, and much hard work turned an innovative idea into the business of her dreams. The industry has developed into perhaps the largest retail mail-order ruffled curtain company in America.

The "idea" was Dorothy Noe's original design for the ruffled curtains she made for her new home at 233 Tanbridge Road, Wilmington, in 1971. She designed the curtains as a complement for the antiques that she and her husband were selling there. People coming to see the antiques were so impressed by the unique curtains that it became obvious the curtains were a marketable commodity. Initially, the demand for the custom-made curtains was met by the developing cottage industry. In 1973-1974, Mrs. Noe decided that Wilmington might not be large enough to support the type of business she visualized, and she ventured into the mail-order field. Advertising quickly expanded to include 23 national and regional magazines and 19 North Carolina and Virginia newspapers.

The volume of mail-order and direct sales increased rapidly, and in 1978 a showroom and separate factory were built on Market Street. Recently the factory was enlarged to double its original size, and a second shift of seamstresses was hired. The 1982 goal is to triple sales volume, employ a third shift of seamstresses, and double the size of the showroom.

The company makes direct retail sales in its six shops—five in North Carolina and one in Williamsburg, Virginia. Additional shops will open soon in Greensboro, North Carolina, and in Washington, D.C., at Georgetown. Approximately 100 persons are now on the payroll, and the contemplated expansions will require hiring 50 or 60 additional employees.

A member of the United States Chamber of Commerce, Dorothy's Ruffled Originals, Inc., does a worldwide business. Regular, extensive advertising has resulted in making the showroom "one of *the* places to see in Wilmington." This is a quote from many tourist visitors, who often make a detour in their travels in order to stop at Mrs. Noe's shop.

Doubtless this expanding operation has had a favorable impact on the local economy, taking into account not only the considerable payroll engendered, but the tourism generated, the impressive advertising budget, and the firm's policy of patronizing local sources whenever possible for supplies and equipment.

Dorothy's Ruffled Original's business has been developed under the premise of supplying a superior product. The reward of this product being so enthusiastically accepted has provided the designer with a tremendous sense of accomplishment, making her grateful to be living in a country that has permitted her the freedom to develop her ideas and make a dream come true. ◆ ◆ ◆

The showroom of Dorothy's Ruffled Originals.

General Electric Company

General Electric's "factory of the future" in Wilmington consists of two high-technology businesses—the Nuclear Energy Business Operation, which manufactures nuclear equipment and nuclear fuel, and the Aircraft Engine Business Group, which manufactures rotating parts for jet engines. The plant site consists of 1,664 acres with 338 acres actually developed for use. With over one million square feet of office and manufacturing space, the firm's 2,400 employees are providing quality products to customers around the world.

After surveying some 80 different sites, Wilmington was selected by the company to be the home of the world's most modern nuclear manufacturing facility. In December 1967 plans were announced locally. On March 29, 1968, the plant was officially opened and through the years the operation has continued to expand.

In April 1980 a satellite plant of General Electric's Aircraft Engine Business Group located in Wilmington to manufacture rotating parts for commercial and military aircraft engines. High-precision parts are produced through the use of state-of-the-art machinery.

Since 1975 the organization has routinely added new manufacturing capability through new investments. Much of this investment has been in automated equipment and computerized systems, along with mini-computers and microprocessors to enhance quality detection and control capability and automatic data acquisition and retention. Wilmington plant inventors have developed nearly 200 patents for the company.

General Electric employees in Wilmington are building a worldwide reputation of progress through quality products and services. They are proud of their team effort in building a unique community within their own plant, working together to develop and manufacture the best products to meet their customers' needs.

With a wide variety of skills, aptitudes, and interests, these General Electric men and women are the reason that the name General Electric is a proud tradition. General Electric is proud to call Wilmington, North Carolina, "home."

An aerial view of the General Electric Nuclear Energy Business Operation and Aircraft Engine Business Group, located in Wilmington.

E.W. Godwin's Sons, Inc.

Four generations of the E.W. Godwin family have operated the retail lumber business in the Wilmington area. The story of this enterprise began in Delaware, where Mr. E.W. Godwin made the decision to go to North Carolina for a look at the lumber industry there. News of a good and fast-growing lumber supply prompted Godwin to travel to eastern North Carolina. He brought along his trusty bicycle to explore the region. In Burgaw someone told him of a sawmill for sale at Rhynes Crossroads in Pender County. After looking at the operation, he decided to purchase the mill and accompanying timberlands. Returning to Delaware, he put his affairs in order and moved his family to North Carolina during Christmas of 1909. Godwin, his wife, and three sons spent the first night in Burgaw, rented a horse and wagon, and proceeded to their new home at Rhynes Crossroads. His enterprises were on the Black River and later on the Northeast River. Water was used to move the logs from the timber sites upriver to the mill. One of the mill sites was at Point Caswell, once a thriving shipping point on Black River. Logs were cut and rafted downriver using a small tugboat to guide the raft.

W.C. Godwin, E.P. Godwin, Sr., and Earl M. Godwin inherited their father's business in 1932. The sons of E.P. Godwin, Sr., are the major stockholders of the company today. Julian W. Godwin is president, Ebe W. Godwin serves as vice-president, and James Z. Godwin is secretary and acting treasurer. E.P. Godwin, Sr., holds the position of honorary treasurer. His grandsons, Jay Godwin, Ebe Godwin, Jr., Zach Godwin, and John Godwin, constitute the fourth generation actively involved in the family business.

The number of employees has grown from about 15 in 1909 to 140 in 1982. The sawmill location is on an eight-acre site at Wallace, but all other aspects of the manufacture are completed at the Castle Hayne Road location. This Smith Creek site consists of 24 acres with 15 buildings and 24 trucks. Here the lumber is dried, graded, dressed, and prepared for shipment. Approximately 16 million feet of pine and some cypress lumber is produced each year. The company does pressure treating and prepares lumber with a fire retardant carrying the underwriter's label. Trusses, window and door units, and other facets of the modern building industry are produced. In the beginning the firm dealt primarily with the production of lumber; for the past 45 years, building materials have contributed a major part.

E.W. Godwin's Sons, Inc., has been active in the trade association field. W.C. Godwin served as president of the Carolina Lumber Dealer's Association. A 75-mile radius is served

◆ ◆ ◆

Below: *The first building on the present plant site of E.W. Godwin's Sons, Inc., on Castle Hayne Road, circa 1929.*

by a business based on service and quality—quality at a price. Four generations of Godwins literally have helped to build southeastern North Carolina.

◆ ◆ ◆

Bottom: *A 1949 aerial view (looking northwest) of the firm's plant site on Castle Hayne Road.*

W.R. Grace & Co.

Located along the northeast Cape Fear River, two miles north of Wilmington, on U.S. Highway 421, are the W.R. Grace & Co. Agricultural Chemicals Group Nitrex plant and regional sales administrative offices. W.R. Grace & Co., founded in 1854 in Peru by William Russell Grace, is an international chemical organization with related natural resources and selected consumer businesses.

The Wilmington facility, a nitrogen-conversion chemical plant, was officially dedicated in 1964 and was one of the first industrial installations contributing to the city's industrial expansion utilizing the northeast Cape Fear River as a deep-water harbor.

Employing inorganic chemistry and engineering technology, the plant converts approximately 100,000 tons of anhydrous ammonia into approximately 300,000 tons of solid and liquid products of ammonia and ammonium nitrate for agricultural markets. The anhydrous ammonia is transported from a Grace plant in Trinidad in the West Indies by special cryogenic ships and is unloaded at plant-docking facilities on the northeast Cape Fear River.

The heart of the Wilmington facility is a nitric acid plant where ammonia is converted into nitric acid. Nitric acid is then converted into ammonium nitrate. Other ingredients used in the agricultural products manufactured are urea, shipped from a Grace plant in Trinidad and unloaded at the North Carolina State Ports

The Wilmington facility of W.R. Grace & Co., a nitrogen-conversion chemical plant.

◆ ◆ ◆

Authority in Wilmington, and minerals, such as diatomaceous earth and kaolin clay.

When completed, the plant design

incorporated the latest technology. Management at the facility has always placed high priority on the maintenance and improvement of reclamation, filtering, scrubbing, and recycling systems to keep pace with changing technology and environmental regulations.

The plant employs approximately 118 people with another 60 to 70 working in and out of the regional sales offices located on the plant site. Fertilizers manufactured at the facility are distributed throughout North and South Carolina, Virginia, and Georgia, as well as portions of adjacent states to be used on cotton, corn, tobacco, hay, and other major crops raised there. To meet farm requirements for balanced and special fertilizer blends, the eastern region operates mixed fertilizer plants in Wilmington and Statesville, North Carolina, and Charleston, South Carolina, and blending plants in Fort Pierce and Tampa, Florida.

On February 13, 1964, the Wilmington plant was dedicated to the welfare and prosperity of southern agriculture and industry. Through the present, W.R. Grace & Co. not only has been dedicated to agriculture but to being an asset to the community and providing year-round employment for its employees.

◆ ◆ ◆

The W.R. Grace & Co. facility was dedicated in 1964 and utilizes the northeast Cape Fear River as a deep-water harbor.

The Lower Cape Fear Historical Society

The Zebulon Latimer House, headquarters of The Lower Cape Fear Historical Society, was built in 1852.

The Lower Cape Fear Historical Society, Inc., this volume's sponsor, was organized on April 28, 1956. As set forth in the incorporation papers, the Society was to " and preserve records and materials an nate knowledge and information per the history of the Lower Cape Fear State of North Carolina, and the Unite of America." In its first year of existenc Society began publishing the *Bulletin*, a jo containing scholarly articles about the histor the lower Cape Fear area. Historic research a publication were to be encouraged with th Clarendon Award to be presented annually by the Society for the best publication pertaining to local history. An annual lecture series was developed to present three noted speakers. A revolving publication fund was established in 1962, to honor the late Cape Fear historian, Louis T. Moore. Since its founding, the Society's archival collection has grown steadily. The Ida B. Kellam Archives Library was officially established in 1967. Mrs. Kellam, the archivist, bequeathed her vast collection of Cape Fear memorabilia to the Society in 1981. The library continues to serve as a tribute to Mrs. Kellam's research and preservation of information pertaining to the area's history.

In December 1963 the Society purchased the architecturally significant Italianate Revival-style Zebulon Latimer House located in Wilmington's historic district. It took four years to raise funds and accomplish the restoration of this wealthy commission merchant's 1852 home. A March 1981 disastrous fire severely damaged this headquarters, but members rose to the occasion and were able

to reopen the house the following November—although the restoration was not yet complete. Original paint hues and the additional restoration of the hall and basement dining room and kitchen add to the interpretation of this house museum, which is part of the Historic Wilmington Tour.

The Lower Cape Fear Historical Society has been involved in and supportive of civic projects which promise to preserve the historical character of the port city. Among the first was sponsorship of Innes Park in front of Thalian Hall. The Society lobbied for and assisted in the creation of the Wilmington Historic District zoning ordinance in 1962. This was one of the state's first historic district ordinances which attempted, through the board of architectural review, to preserve the character of the old residential section of downto Wilmington. Three years later the money to sponsor the historic area ociety ation mer ng e

Candlelight, was established. In recognition of the significance of the project, the National Park Service awarded grants of $16,000.

Future plans include continuing research and publication, completion and interpretation of the Latimer House restoration, expansion of the Archives, and restoration of the grounds of the headquarters. An Incorporator's Garden has been approved to honor Ida B. Kellam, Hargrove Bellamy, and Henry J. Mac-Millan for their foresight in establishing this viable organization for the preservation of our heritage.

The Lower Cape Fear Historical Society's important contributions in the fields of historical research, publication, and preservation were recognized by the state of North Carolina in 1976 by the presentation of the Ruth Coltrane Cannon Cup, North Carolina's most prestigious preservation award.

Signing of the deed to the Latimer House in 1963. Seated (left to right) are Herbert Latimer, from whom the house was purchased; Winfield Sapp, president; and Leila Stack, secretary. Standing are other officers of the Society. (Photo courtesy of Southeastern Engraving Company.)

North Carolina State Ports Authority

An *aerial view of the State Port of Wilmington.*

N orth Carolina's rich nautical heritage led farsighted citizens during the 1920s to ask their state government to develop the ports of the state. Federal assistance from the Army Corps of Engineers kept channels dredged and harbors clear of obstruction. World War I had brought new emphasis to the viability of the ports, and citizen pressure began to build for a state government commitment to develop them. It was not until 1945, however, that the North Carolina Ports Authority was created by the General Assembly. It was commissioned to contribute to the economic growth of the state through development and maintenance of modern and efficient port facilities. A 1949 law further defined the job of the Authority to develop and improve the harbors and seaports of North Carolina for a more expeditious and effective handling of water-borne commerce to and from any place or places in the state and other states and foreign countries.

Today manufactured goods and raw materials from around the world enter and leave the United States through North Carolina's state-owned deep-water ports at Wilmington and Morehead City. Nearly 800 vessels now call each year. Among the nation's leaf tobacco export centers, the ports typically ship about 350 million pounds. U.S. Customs maintains offices at both terminals, with clearance usually in 24 hours.

The citizens of North Carolina are the shareholders in this governmental entity, which has increased tonnage during the past two decades more than thirtyfold. The Authority promotes international trade and economic development as exhibited by the flags of nations from every continent that pass through the terminals, their ships bearing the world's goods.

At Wilmington, the terminal is located 26 miles from the mouth of the Cape Fear River. The channel and turning basins are maintained at a depth of 38 feet mean low water, where the famous pilots of the river have guided their vessels to the moorings for more than 200 years. A marginal wharf of 6,000 feet with double railroad tracks assures rapid cargo handling. Storage facilities include 1.5 million square feet of sprinkler-equipped interior space and 60 acres of paved exterior area. Two 40-ton full-bridge container cranes and additional gantry and mobile cranes are in use. Seaboard Coast Line and over 50 motor carriers, many maintaining Wilmington terminals, provide transit. Tonnage has increased to nearly three million tons per year. The Port of Wilmington is a designated Foreign Trade Zone offering warehouse and cargo space and 13 acres for use as special custom zones.

Because of the Port of Wilmington's growth, the North Carolina State Ports Authority board of directors has approved a $12-million expansion program. Container storage and handling capability will increase by 75 percent and an additional container crane will be purchased. The new terminal will be constructed on a 33-acre site directly south of the present 50-acre container facility. SPA executive director William M.A. Greene called the decision "one of the most important developments to ever happen at the State Ports Authority." Considering its size, Wilmington has the fastest growing terminal on the East Coast and is being recognized as "*the* port authority."

◆ ◆ ◆

Sea-Land, the largest container line in the world, now offers service at the Port of Wilmington.

Oleander Company, Inc.

Hugh MacRae II, president of Oleander Company, Inc., continues to serve the people and community of Wilmington as did his grandfather, Hugh MacRae.

The story of Oleander Company, Inc., has its origin with president Hugh MacRae II's namesake and grandfather, Hugh MacRae. MacRae had founded the large holding enterprise Hugh MacRae and Company in 1924 with offices in the MacRae Building on Front Street in Wilmington. Oleander Company was established under the auspices of Hugh MacRae and Company for the general development of real estate, particularly Wilmington's eastern

suburban area extending to Wrightsville Beach. Oleander Company, subsequently Oleander Company, Inc., was responsible for the first major suburban development in Wilmington, one of the earliest in the United States. An affiliate enterprise, Linville Improvement Company, was involved with the development of Grandfather Mountain and Linville, North Carolina. Hugh MacRae and Company continued with development of Castle Hayne and Wrightsville Beach, coal mining in Virginia, farming, and timberlands.

From 1924 to 1951 Hugh MacRae served as chairman of the board of Hugh MacRae and Company. Presidents, respectively, of the firms under him were his son, Nelson MacRae, 1924 to 1942; his son-in-law, Julian Morton, 1943 to 1945; and his grandson, Hugh MacRae Morton, 1945 to 1951. Hugh MacRae and Company was dissolved upon its chairman's death in 1951.

Oleander Company, Inc., continued most of the Wilmington operations in 1952, when Nelson MacRae's son, Hugh MacRae II, became president of the enterprise. Hugh MacRae II has operated with acumen under a premise established by his grandfather. MacRae's policy was that his primary motive in business was to produce projects and developments that would serve the people and make Wilmington and North Carolina a better place to live. He felt that profit was secondary and would be a side benefit. Oleander Company has developed South Oleander, Oleander Estates, Forest Hills extension, Piney Woods, Echo

Farms, Lincoln Forest, Hanover Center, and Independence Mall. As the organization evolved, the office was moved to its current location at 3501 Oleander Drive—closer to the area it develops.

Hugh MacRae II's civic involvements express his interest in supporting the development and improvement of Wilmington and the Historic District. These are best exemplified by his service as a member of the planning commission that established the Historic District, vice-chairman of Bellamy Mansion, Inc., vice-chairman of the St. James Episcopal Church building campaign in 1956, key to acquisition of his great-uncle Donald MacRae's house for use as St. James Church offices, and member of the Historic Wilmington Foundation. He served as chairman of the board of James Walker Memorial Hospital, turned the first shovel for development of the New Hanover Memorial Hospital, and donated land for and built a road to serve St. John's Episcopal Church. He was on the board that decided to locate Wachovia Bank downtown, anchoring financial business there, and he has served on the board of Wachovia since 1956. MacRae gave early assistance in the establishment of the North Carolina State Ports Authority and the formulation of Plans for I-40 Highway connection to Wilmington. He continues with discernment the tradition established by his grandfather.

Independence Mall, one of the many developments of the Oleander Company, Inc.

Richardson Corporation

Lunsford Richardson, Sr., founder of Vick Chemical Company.

Early in this century Lunsford Richardson and his two sons, Smith and Lunsford Jr., had transformed their small pharmacy and wholesale drug business into the thriving Vick Chemical Company. The only product at that time was Vicks VapoRub, then as now a very successful and fast-selling remedy for the symptoms of cold and flu. Sales volume doubled each year for several years during the 1915-1920 period and the company opened international branches in the early 1920s.

In 1925 the decision was made to sell stock to the general public in a business that heretofore had been wholly owned by the members of the Richardson family. As was common in those days, Vick Chemical Company had invested unneeded capital in real estate, principally in the Greensboro area, and, when the company went public, these real estate assets were spun off to create Richardson Corporation of Greensboro.

For years, Richardson Corporation served as a Richardson family holding company, managing the properties, brokering transactions, and assisting family members with their own real estate investments. Gradually these services were offered to the public and Richardson Corporation became a full-fledged real estate brokerage, management, and construction firm by the late 1930s. An insurance agency was acquired in 1949, adding the capabilities of an independent insurance firm.

The scale of activities increased throughout the '60s, and by the early '80s Richardson Corporation was doing business across the state. It acquired the Hardy Wessell Insurance Agency in Wilmington in 1975, and early in 1976 the Clayton-Beall Insurance Agency as well. These established firms had served the lower Cape Fear region for a number of years and were able to enhance their services by the resources of Richardson Corporation. The Wilmington insurance division is located in its own building at 319 Walnut Street.

Four years later, in 1979, a real estate brokerage division office was established; it now occupies an office in a shopping center rehabilitated by Richardson Corporation on Oleander Drive in Wilmington.

Through these two division offices, Richardson's complete range of services is available to the Wilmington community. The staff serves in the capacities of all five divisions: real estate brokerage, construction, real estate management, real estate investment and counseling, and insurance. This extensive range of services, staffed by full-time professionals at every level, is what distinguishes Richardson Corporation from others in its field. Richardson Corporation and its subsidiaries operate real estate and insurance firms throughout the Carolinas and the array of its services and the range of its experience are available to every client.

Above: *Corporate headquarters of Richardson Corporation, One Southern Life Center, Greensboro.*

Below: *An Early Vick Chemical Company factory.*

Z.A. Sneeden's Sons, Inc.

Z. A. Sneeden founded his grading and utility contracting company in 1910, based on a foundation that his word was his bond. His two favorite axioms were "The harder you work, the luckier you get," and, "If you want to live better than average, you have to gamble; if you don't gamble, you'll scratch a poor man's back all your life." He maintained a belief in free enterprise and wanted to establish himself as a sound businessman.

His first office was combined with a shop and equipment on Oleander Drive near Seagate. From the onset of the Depression until 1945, the office was located in the Odd Fellow's Building at Third and Princess streets. Sneeden constructed an office building at 16th and Wooster streets in 1945. During his first year of business he employed a dozen people, paying the average wage of a dollar a day; mules and pans were the equipment of the time.

One of the firm's early contracts was for building the first streets on Wrightsville Beach. Sneeden used the mules and pans to grade present-day Lumina Avenue from Station One north. Since there was no vehicular bridge connecting Wrightsville, mules and equipment were transported in boxcars by Tide Water Power Company, operator of the trolley to the beach. The firm graded other streets at Wrightsville, in Wilmington, and throughout the state. When Dow Chemical Company moved to Wilmington in the 1930s, Sneeden obtained a grading contract with the corporation, a major job during the Depression. During the post-World War II years, Sneeden became actively involved as a grading and utilities contractor due to the construction of Camp Davis, Camp Lejeune, and the Wilmington Shipyard. The paving industry was developing at that time, also.

Sneeden instilled in his sons his pioneer spirit; and, upon completion of their military service, he encouraged their business interest and began giving them stock in the company. After the demise of Z.A. Sneeden in 1951, his four sons—Jack A., E.B., D.W., and T.W.—continued the firm's operation.

During the late '50s and early '60s the sons divided responsibilities and established separate enterprises. T.W. Sneeden and E.B. Sneeden opened Hanover Company and deal mainly with grading and paving. D.W. Sneeden established Lincoln Construction Company, a heavy-grading business. Jack A. Sneeden continued to operate Z.A. Sneeden's Sons, Inc.

Today Z.A. Sneeden's Sons does commercial building and developing. The office building at 721 Market Street, K mart Shopping Center, and National Outlet Shopping Center are a few of the developments in Wilmington completed by the firm. The company constructs and owns shopping centers and offices throughout North Carolina.

Jack A. Sneeden emulates his father's pioneer liveliness in his business expertise. Suite 402 in the Wachovia Bank Building serves as office headquarters. He and his wife Elnora are president and secretary of the company, respectively. Their son Jack A. Sneeden, Jr., is vice-president in charge of leasing. The company, well into the third generation, will be joined by the Sneedens' younger son, Stuart, and their daughter, Gretta. Jack A. Sneeden's interests are not limited to his business; he has served on the board of trustees of Meredith College in Raleigh for nearly 20 years. His religious involvement has included serving on the board of deacons and holding various offices of the First Baptist Church of Wilmington.

Z.A. Sneeden, founder of Z.A. Sneeden's Sons, Inc.

The University of North Carolina at Wilmington

The fastest growing four-year public or private college in the state, The University of North Carolina at Wilmington is proud of its role as a regional center of higher learning, as a cultural center, and as a strong contributor to the area's economy.

Looking back, it's not quite clear who first expressed a need for a college in the Wilmington area. According to the *Wilmington Star-News*, the idea for such an institution was conceived in the late 1930s by the New Hanover County Board of Education. However, because of lack of funds and the dark clouds of World War II, serious consideration had to be postponed. Yet the concept remained active in the minds of John T. Hoggard and H.M. Roland, chairman of the board of education and superintendent of schools, respectively. The first official act leading to the creation of a college occurred on March 21, 1945, when the General Assembly of North Carolina enacted House Bill No. 892, providing for the establishment of a junior college in New Hanover County. With the approval of a tax levy by citizens of the county in 1947, Wilmington College was brought into existence as a county institution under the auspices of the New Hanover County Board of Education.

On September 4, 1947, at 4:00 p.m., Wilmington College, with 17 faculty members and classroom space borrowed in the afternoon from New Hanover High School, opened its doors to 258 students. The next year it moved across Market Street and remained in the Isaac Bear Building until 1961. Thomas T. Hamilton, president from 1947 to 1949, helped to organize and lead the college in its infancy, when veterans provided 75 percent of the student body. John T. Hoggard served as president from 1951 until 1958, when he became chairman of an appointed board of trustees under the Com-

munity College Act of the state. Under the supervision of the North Carolina Board of Higher Education, Wilmington College began to receive an appropriation from the state as a supplement to the local tax levy. On July 1, 1963, the college became a senior-level institution authorized to offer the baccalaureate degree. During the leadership of Dr. William M. Randall, president from 1958 until his retirement in 1968, the college grew to 1,200 students and moved to a 600-acre site on Highway 132, midway between the Cape Fear River and the Atlantic Ocean. Dr. William H. Wagoner then became president of the college in 1968. A year later he was named chancellor when the legislature officially made Wilmington College a part of the Consolidated University of North Carolina and renamed it The University of North Carolina at Wilmington.

The Consolidated University of North Carolina, after its reorganization in 1971, currently is comprised of 16 senior state-supported institutions and is governed by a 32-member board of governors. In 1977 the board authorized UNCW to offer its first graduate programs at the master's level.

UNCW's 1981-1982 enrollment reached 5,000, with graduate programs now offered in the fields of education, marine biology, and business administration. During his term as chancellor, Dr. Wagoner has witnessed major growth in enrollment, expansion of facilities, sports programs, research development, and cultural arts. Enhanced by its strategic coastal location, the university has earned international recognition for excellence in marine-related research. On May 31, 1982, it christened the *Research Vessel Seahawk* to conduct scientific research expeditions along the East Coast.

A wide variety of intercollegiate athletic

programs for men and women is available, and UNCW belongs to major national intercollegiate athletic associations. Kenan Auditorium and Trask Coliseum, the area's largest meeting facility, provide a center for activities including theater, university performing ensembles in music, lectures, and conventions, as well as performances by the North Carolina Symphony and national and international artists.

The university's most significant achievements have been growth of an excellent faculty, expansion of physical facilities, and an increase in the variety and number of cultural and educational offerings. The University of North Carolina at Wilmington is committed to equality of educational opportunities and does not discriminate against applicants, students, or employees based on race, color, national origin, religion, sex, age, or handicap. Moreover, The University of North Carolina at Wilmington is open to people of all races and actively seeks to promote racial integration by recruiting and enrolling a larger number of black students.

◆ ◆ ◆

Left: *Aerial view of The University of North Carolina at Wilmington campus taken in 1962 shortly after the three new buildings were first occupied. Today 27 buildings are either in use or under construction plus 13 student apartment buildings and athletic fields.*

Right: *With a 6,600-seat capacity, Trask Coliseum is the largest meeting place in Southeastern North Carolina. As a result of extensive community support in a fund-raising campaign, air conditioning, installed in late 1982, now allows the building to be used for the year-round programming of public service and cultural programs, concerts, trade shows, and community events, including the annual Azalea Festival.*

Wachovia Bank and Trust Company, N.A.

Organized banking came to North Carolina in 1804, when the General Assembly chartered the state's first two banks: the Bank of Cape Fear in Wilmington, and the New Bern Bank. Expansion came slowly, and it was not until 1815 that Piedmont residents gained access to banking services, when the Bank of Cape Fear opened an agency in Salem. The War Between the States brought the collapse of all North Carolina banks, and many—including the Bank of Cape Fear—never reopened.

Israel G. Lash, a former cashier of the Bank of Cape Fear, obtained a charter, and in 1866 opened the First National Bank of Salem. Community growth shifted to nearby Winston. Following Lash's death, his nephew William A. Lemly closed the Salem bank, packed its safe and furnishings and moved "uptown" to Winston. Changing towns required a new charter and hence a new name. On June 16, 1879, the doors opened on the new Wachovia National Bank. "Wachovia" is an anglicized version of "Wachau," the name chosen by the Moravians in 1752 to describe the North Carolina land where they built their settlements.

The North Carolina General Assembly voted in 1891 to charter a new form of financial institution called the "trust company." On June 15, 1893, North Carolina's first trust company, Wachovia Loan and Trust Company, opened for business in Winston. Within 10 years it was the largest financial institution in North Carolina. In 1910 the decision was made to merge Wachovia National Bank and Wachovia Loan and Trust Company.

A strong, consolidated Wachovia Bank and Trust Company opened its doors on January 1, 1911, as the largest bank in the South and the largest trust operation between Baltimore and New Orleans. During the depths of the Depression, Wachovia president Robert M. Hanes, accompanied by guards, took a suitcase full of cash to one Wachovia office and opened it in the lobby to show customers that the firm would weather the financial crisis.

In 1955 Wachovia merged with People's Savings and Trust of Wilmington, a bank that had been in operation since 1900. Another merger took place in 1958 with the Wilmington Savings and Trust Company, which had been serving citizens since 1888. Wachovia was the first bank in North Carolina to create an international department. It was started in 1960 in Wilmington to serve the international banking needs of the port city.

Wachovia's Wilmington office has over 100 employees. William H. Joyner, Jr., a banker for 26 years, serves as office executive. The bank has retail, corporate, personnel, sales finance, mortgage, and trust departments. In addition to the main office located on the Cape Fear River, there are five branch offices in Wilmington.

The Wachovia Corporation, headquartered in Winston-Salem, North Carolina, is a one-bank holding company with three subsidiaries engaged in banking and banking-related financial services. Wachovia Bank and Trust Company, N.A., comprises the vast majority of the business, complemented by Wachovia Mortgage Company and Wachovia Services, Inc.

Wachovia Bank provides personal, commercial, trust, and institutional banking services through 196 offices in 81 North Carolina cities and towns. In addition, it has a foreign branch at Grand Cayman, an Edge Act bank in New York City, and representative offices in New York City and Zurich. Retail banking is conducted primarily through the statewide branch network, but other services are provided to corporations and institutions across North Carolina, the Southeast, the nation, and the world.

◆ ◆ ◆

Wilmington headquarters of Wachovia Bank and Trust Company, N.A., located at North Front and Princess streets, 1960.

Walker Taylor-Insurance

Colonel Walker Taylor.

Walker Taylor III receives a 100th anniversary plaque from Isaac Grainger, director, and Ray Gardner, manager, of Hartford Fire Insurance Company.

◆ ◆ ◆

The slogan Colonel Walker Taylor originated for his insurance agency was "Insurance, That's All." He was 14 when he left school and became an office boy for the old DeRosset & Northrop Agency. "The fairies that hovered over his baby cradle," said a biographical sketch published in a New York periodical on the occasion of his 50th anniversary in the insurance business, "were not generous with Colonel Taylor in worldly goods, but they gave him instead a strong body, a clear brain, and a stout heart. In those days, the office boy literally 'cleaned the windows and swept the floor and polished up the handle on the big front door.' But meanwhile, he was making himself into a high-type insurance broker and very early in life he established his own business. . . ."

Born in 1864, and raised during the dismal days following the Civil War, Colonel Taylor prospered through the sheer force of work, uncompromising integrity, and prudent living. He was a director of Murchison National Bank, Peoples Savings Bank, and Tide Water Power Company; founder of Cooperative Savings & Loan Association; and founder of Jefferson Standard Life Insurance Company with his friend Julian Price. As the unbearded patriarch of Wilmington, his advice was solicited by young and old alike. On February 14, 1896, he founded the Boys' Brigade, forerunner of boys' clubs in America. Colonel Taylor was a ruling elder of First Presbyterian Church. He refused public office, with the exception of the solicitation of President Woodrow Wilson to become

United States Collector of Customs in 1913. In a letter to his brother Edward, dated September 19, 1895, Colonel Taylor gave such maxims for successful employment as "You can learn something every day, if you try. . . . When you have nothing to say, hold your tongue. . . . When you slip up, own up. . . ." During World War II, the Liberty ship S.S. *Walker Taylor* was named for Colonel Taylor.

In 1878 Colonel Taylor joined the 1866 insurance firm of DeRosset & Northrop and later purchased the business. In 1919, after graduation from Princeton University, his son Walker Taylor, Jr., joined the organization and developed the casualty insurance business because of the advent of the automobile. In 1948 Walker Taylor III joined the firm after graduation from Davidson College and the U.S. Merchant Marine Academy. John Van B. Metts, Jr., joined Walker Taylor-Insurance as a partner in 1951. The agency started developing marine insurance under Metts' leadership and is now the largest marine broker in North Carolina. Upon the death of Walker Taylor, Jr., in 1963, Walker Taylor III and J. Van B. Metts, Jr., continued as partners until Taylor purchased Metts' interest in 1982.

Walker Taylor III received an honorary doctor's degree from Berkeley at Yale for his work with the Domestic and Foreign Missionary Society of the Episcopal Church. He served on

the board of trustees of the University of the South, General Theological Seminary, and Berkeley Divinity School, and was chairman of the finance committee of the Episcopal Church for six years. He is chairman of the local board of Wachovia Bank and Trust Company.

"Insurance, That's All" remains the slogan of this third-generation agency representing Hartford Fire and Aetna Insurance since 1878, German American since 1896 (known as Great American since World War I), Chubb since 1896, Home since 1906, and numerous other underwriters for many years.

◆ ◆ ◆

Ship's bell and name plate from the S.S. Walker Taylor.

S.S. WALKER TAYLOR
BUILT FOR
U.S. MARITIME COMMISSION
HULL NO. 902
BY
NORTH CAROLINA SHIPBUILDING COMPANY
WILMINGTON, NORTH CAROLINA
MARCH 1943

Wilmington Coca-Cola Bottling Works, Inc.

The Coca-Cola success story is a southern one. From the most humble of beginnings in Atlanta, Coca-Cola moved out of the South, across America, and then throughout the world to become, as the company publications like to point out, the best-known trademark on earth. The confectionary odor of sugar and water in mixture to make Coca-Cola syrup is the sweet smell of an extraordinary success providing 200 million drinks to the people of this earth every day.

At about the same time that Dr. John Pemberton was creating Coca-Cola in Atlanta, George Henry Hutaff was experimenting with and bottling grape and orange drinks in his backyard in Wilmington. Hutaff would take his pushcart and go from house to house offering his drinks for sale. He would wait for the purchaser to enjoy the drink and then return the bottle for future use. A most ingenious man, Hutaff also grew lettuce and strawberries in the Castle Hayne area near Wilmington and experimented with a large-scale freezing operation for shipping vegetables.

During Coca-Cola's early years, Hutaff made an important decision. He signed a contract for a Coca-Cola franchise in September 1902. Thus Wilmington Coca-Cola Bottling Works was incorporated on July 10, 1909, with George Henry Hutaff, his wife Tabitha, and his brother W.J. Hutaff as shareholders. All shares of the company have always been owned by these family members, their children, and their grandchildren. Hutaff also assisted another brother in Fayetteville in obtaining a franchise.

The operation was moved to its current location at 921 Princess Street in 1914. The original plant could annually produce less than 50,000 cases. The drinks were prepared with the Coca-Cola syrup first received in 54-gallon wooden drums, later in steel drums, and presently in tanker trucks holding 4,500 gallons. In the peak summer season, two tankers often deliver daily. Today three bottling lines can provide over eight million cases annually.

From 1902 to 1957, the corporation produced only coke in a 6.5-ounce glass bottle. Now 6.5-, 10-, 16-, 28-, and 32-ounce bottles, 12-ounce cans, and .5- and 2-liter plastic bottles are available. Other allied products manufactured are Sprite, Fanta Grape and Orange, Tab, Santiba, and Fresca. Early distribution was by horse and buggy and by rail car; now the familiar beverage truck delivers.

From 1956 to 1980 the business grew and prospered under the leadership of George Henry Hutaff's son, Oliver C. Hutaff. The plant was completely remodeled and expanded between 1965 and 1972. It is now the largest Coca-Cola manufacturing plant in eastern North Carolina, employing 150 people. The firm also produces for Electric Bottling Company and for Coca-Cola plants in New Bern, Rocky Mount, Kelford, Weldon, and Emporia, Virginia. It owns part of the canning co-op South Atlantic Canners in Bishopville, South Carolina, and has an interest in the vending company Food Service, Inc., in Columbia, South Carolina.

The vision of George Henry Hutaff led him on the fantastic adventure of building the Wilmington Coca-Cola Bottling Works. This family enterprise has developed into quite a success story over the years and current officers Oliver C. Hutaff, Jr., Tabitha Hutaff McEachern, and Emma Gade Hutaff carry on the long tradition.

Children of George Henry and W.J. Hutaff with their relative, Richard Cromwell.

Wright Chemical Corporation

Wright Chemical Corporation is a locally owned producer of selected industrial chemicals. Its manufacturing facilities are located at Acme in Columbus County, 20 miles west of Wilmington, North Carolina. The company started operations in February 1959, when it opened a small liquid alum plant. This plant used sulfuric acid and Alabama bauxite to manufacture alum for use in waterworks of nearby municipalities and in paper mills of the area. Wright Chemical later merged with Acme Chemicals, Inc., a chamber process sulfuric acid plant. This plant was the outgrowth of the acid plant started in 1883 by William Gilchrist, founder of Acme Fertilizer Company and grandfather of Thomas H. Wright, Jr., founder of Wright Chemical Corporation.

In 1964 the company built a Monsanto-Leonard-designed contact sulfuric acid plant and widened its sales of sulfuric acid to industrial customers of the area, as well as furnishing its alum plant. During the same year a joint venture, known as Ross-Wright Chemical Corporation, was formed with F.H. Ross & Company of Charlotte. This enterprise constructed and operated two liquid alum plants at Cedar Springs, Georgia, and at Fernandina Beach, Florida. These plants were sold to Cities Service Company in 1969.

Wright Chemical Corporation entered the urea-formaldehyde adhesive business in 1967, with the construction of an adhesive plant at Acme. A formaldehyde plant was built there the same year. Two additional formaldehyde units were built at Acme in March and November 1968. These units were built by the company's staff. A hexamine plant of the firm's design began operation in January 1967. The initial contract was to furnish the U.S. Army with hexamine for use in making explosives; however, the output of the plant now goes to a wide range of industrial uses. A major expansion in the urea-formaldehyde adhesive business was completed in the winter of 1970 with the construction of a UF plant and a formaldehyde unit at Malvern, Arkansas, and a UF plant at Waverly, Virginia. A methanol storage terminal was built in Pine Bluff, Arkansas, in addition to the one operated by the company in Wilmington, North Carolina. This made the Wright Chemical Corporation a major adhesive supplier to the growing particle board industry in the southeastern United States.

In 1973 the Malvern operation was sold to Reichhold Chemicals, Inc., the Waverly plant to Spurlock Company, and the Acme adhesive plant was closed. The firm continued to emphasize its production and sales of sulfuric acid, hexamine, and formaldehyde. In 1976, and in 1981-1982, it made major expansions and improvements to its sulfuric acid and hexamine plants. Furthering its growth, Wright Chemical Corporation entered into the production of decontaminants.

In June 1976 Wright Chemical Company diversified its interests with the purchase of land for tourism development on the Cape Fear River at Wilmington between Ann and Nun streets. This was the beginning of the shopping, dining, and museum complex known as Chandler's Wharf. During the next two years the complex acquired a 147-foot two-masted wooden schooner (constructed in Lunenberg, Nova Scotia, in 1937) and four other vessels to be used in its Marine Museum. Five small endangered residential buildings were moved to the complex for use as a restaurant and retail stores, and a central warehouse building was constructed. Chandler's Wharf opened in May 1978, and during the following year 18th- and 19th-century warehouses across the street were adapted for use as retail stores and an architectural office.

Wright Chemical Company's founder, Thomas H. Wright, Jr., is now chairman of the board of directors; Newton J. Kelly, who has been with the organization since 1934, is president; William E. Oakley is executive vice-president; and Thomas H. Wright III is secretary, carrying on the family tradition.

◆ ◆ ◆

Acme Manufacturing Company's sulfuric acid plant, circa 1912.

Patrons

The following individuals, companies, and organizations have made a valuable commitment to the quality of this publication. Windsor Publications and The Lower Cape Fear Historical Society gratefully acknowledge their participation in *Cape Fear Adventure: An Illustrated History of Wilmington*.

ATC Petroleum, Inc.*
Atlantic Telecasting Corporation*
Bland & Associates, REALTORS, Better
    Homes and Gardens*
Mr. and Mrs. Charles H. Boney
Carolina Bottlers, Inc.*
Carolina Power & Light Company*
Cherry, Bekaert & Holland*
D. & L. Trucking Inc.*
Dorothy's Ruffled Originals, Inc.*
E.I. du Pont Co., Cape Fear Site

F.P. Fensel Supply Company
General Electric Company*
E.W. Godwin's Sons, Inc.*
Godwin Oil Co. Inc.
W.R. Grace & Co.*
Hanover Urological Associates, P.A.
Historic St. Thomas Preservation Society, Inc.
Dr. & Mrs. Joseph W. Hooper, Jr.
Mr. & Mrs. Oliver C. Hutaff, Jr.
Jackson Beverage Company, Inc.
Mr. and Mrs. Robert A. Little
Tabitha Hutaff McEachern
Hugh MacRae II
Murray, Staton & Fisher
North Carolina State Ports Authority*
Oleander Company, Inc.*
The Oleander Garden Club
Dr. Tilghman Poole
Richardson Corporation*
Mrs. Margaret D.L. Rorison

Service, Inc.
Z.A. Sneeden's Sons, Inc.*
Sutton Council Furniture Co.
Mr. & Mrs. John T. Talbert, Jr.
Mr. and Mrs. C. Heide Trask
The University of North Carolina at
    Wilmington*
Wachovia Bank and Trust Company, N.A.*
Walker Taylor-Insurance*
Waters Shipping Co.
Mrs. Frederick Willett, Jr.
Wilmington Coca-Cola Bottling Works, Inc.*
Wilmington Iron Works
Wright Chemical Corporation*

*Partners in Progress of *Cape Fear Adventure: An Illustrated History of Wilmington*. The histories of these companies and organizations appear in Chapter 8, beginning on page 113.

About the Contributors

James Robert Warren, the author of "Partners in Progress," is a graduate of Virginia Episcopal School and the University of North Carolina. Mr. Warren is a grade-five teacher at Wilmington's oldest school, Tileston.

As a pioneer of historic preservation in Wilmington's historic district, Mr. Warren has preserved his 1840 residence and provided leadership as a founder and first president of the Residents of Old Wilmington, president of the Lower Cape Fear Historical Society, board member of the Historic Wilmington Foundation, originator and chairman of the Wassail Bowl and Old Wilmington by Candlelight tour of private homes, director of the Historic Wilmington Tour, and restoration chairman of the Latimer House Museum. He received the Lower Cape Fear Historical Society's Clarendon Award for his article about Wilmington history, featured in the December 1980 issue of the magazine *Antiques.*

Photographer Freda Hartness Wilkins is a native North Carolinian, and at age 10 was developing her own pictures in her father's darkroom in Sanford. Her avocation became a vocation when she opened her own studio in Wilmington. She studied photography at the University of North Carolina at Raleigh and Wilmington.

Mrs. Wilkins is equally accomplished with black-and-white and color film, and she enjoys both still and action photography. Her freelance credits include advertising and public relations work as well as photographing fast-action sailboat racing. She is the official photographer of the Cape Fear Garden Club and the Auxiliary to the Medical Society of New Hanover, Pender, and Brunswick Counties.

Her prize-winning photos have appeared in juried exhibitions and have been published in "The North Carolina Garden Club Engagement Calendar," and the cookbook, *A Cook's Tour of the Azalea Coast.* Mrs. Wilkins' contributions to this volume include the 16-page color photo essay, as well as many of the fine black-and-white photographs of Wilmington sights.

Pictorial researcher Lynn W. Graham majored in history at the University of South Carolina. This interest led her to Colonial Williamsburg where she trained to become a Colonial Hostess in the Exhibition Building. When she came to Wilmington in 1971 she put her Williamsburg training to good use by helping to develop the New Hanover County Museum's Colonial Youth Program. She served on the Junior League of Wilmington's committee, which implemented this program, and served as an advisor throughout the program's existence. As a result of this work she was appointed to serve as a member of the Board of Trustees of the New Hanover County Museum. Mrs. Graham currently serves as Assistant Archivist of the Lower Cape Fear Historical Society.

Sources

Many people contributed to my research by answering questions, sharing information, and lending privately owned materials. Their generosity enhanced *Cape Fear Adventure* and I would like to thank them— R.V. Asbury, Heyward Bellamy, Hannah Block, Charles H. and Betty H. Boney, Leslie N. and Lillian B. Boney, Mary B. Broadfoot, James Burns, Peter Braak, Sarah J. Bradshaw, Bruce B. Cameron, Daniel Cameron, Catherine Carpender, James O. and Rosalie W. Carr, Harry Cherry, Ed Danilowicz, John H. Debnam, Marshall DesChamps, Joseph and Josephine B. Dunn, Ann Brown Durham, J. Lloyd Durham, Hubert Eaton, Sr., Robert M. Fales, Ralph L. Godwin, Mary M. Gornto, Charles P. and Jean McKoy Graham, Frederick B. and Catherine C. Graham, Herbert D. Hale, Carolyn H. Hall, Frank B. Hall, Margaret T. Hall, Andrew H. Harriss, Jr., Crockette W. Hewlett, Glenn Willard Higgins, Joseph W. and Nell Trask Hooper, Louise Smallbones Hooper, Katherine Howell, Oliver and Ann Bergen Hutaff, Josephine Metts Huntt, Virginia Nesbitt Jennewein, Henry Lee, Henry Jay MacMillan, Hugh MacRae II, Bobbie Marcroft, E.M. and Leora H. McEachern, Elizabeth B. McKoy, Melton McLaurin, Jessie Harper Newboldt, Carl J. Oldenbuttel, Margaret Moore Perdew, Rose Allen Picot, Marilyn Pierce, Dorothy Ray, Bill Reaves, Henry B. Rehder, Jane deRosset Rhett, Tony Rivenbark, Margaret D.L. Rorison, Peter Browne Ruffin, Anne Russell, Janet Seapker, Laura H.N. Schorr, David H. Scott, Alice Moore Sisson, Bess Newton Smith, Elizabeth L. Sprunt, Allan T. Strange, Elizabeth Whitehead Taylor, Walker Taylor III, Beverley Tetterton, Edith Bolles, Graham Toms, Mary Eunice Troy, C. Heide Trask, Miriam M. Warshauer, Alan D. Watson, Mary Hannis Whitted, Cherry Woodbury, and Thomas H. and Elizabeth L. Wright.

North Carolinians have long enjoyed the excellent manuscript collections and resources available at the State of North Carolina's Department of Cultural Resources, Division of Archives and History at Raleigh, the Southern Historical Collection at the University of North Carolina at Chapel Hill Library, and the Flowers Collection at Duke University at Durham; however, the Lower Cape Fear also provides the student of history with comprehensive collections of materials in its local institutions.

The North Carolina Room of the New Hanover County Library contains microfilmed copies of newspapers, official records, private collections, and many books on local history. The William Madison Randall Library of the University of North Carolina at Wilmington has a good local history collection, including the cross-indexed reference file of Civil War materials which was compiled by Leora H. McEachern and Isabel M. Williams, as well as many theses and dissertations written about the region. The Ida Brooks Kellam Memorial Archives of the Lower Cape Fear Historical Society housed at Latimer House, 126 So. Third Street, Wilmington, has a considerable collection of local genealogy, church and club histories, scrapbooks, and letters and diaries of local residents.

Thalian Hall has developed an Archives and Museum, and has Isabel M. Williams' "Report to the Thalian Hall Commission," which is the best documented history of the City Hall-Thalian Hall complex. The Cape Fear Technical Institute has also built a local history collection and is building a park which will demonstrate salt making and turpentine distilling. The New Hanover County Museum emphasizes regional history in its permanent and changing exhibits and most properties participating in the Historic Wilmington Tour also have collections of local interest.

In addition the Cameron Education Building Library at New Hanover Memorial Hospital contains the videotapes of Robert M. Fales, M.D. which present an oral-visual series based on Dr. Fales' collection of over 900 old photographs of Wilmington. Other displays and collections to aid in the understanding of the Lower Cape Fear's past can be found at Old Brunswick Town State Historic Site, Moore's Creek Battlefield National Park, Fort Fisher State Park, Blockade Runners of the Confederacy Museum, and Poplar Grove Plantation.

My research for *Cape Fear Adventure* came from many sources, including official records and newspapers, but the following materials were of particular help.

At the William Madison Randall Library at the University of North Carolina at Wilmington:

Beeker, Henry J. "Wilmington During the Civil War." Master's thesis, Duke University, 1941.

Brewer, James H. "An Account of Negro Slavery in the Cape Fear Region Prior to 1860." Ph.D. dissertation, University of Pittsburgh, 1949.

Loftfield, Thomas C. "A Briefe and True Report, An Archaeological Interpretation of the Southern North Carolina Coast." Ph.D. dissertation, University of North Carolina at Chapel Hill, 1970.

Kornegay, Ralph B. "The Wilmington Riot: November 10, 1898." Master's thesis, Appalachian State University, 1969.

McDuffie, Jerome A. "Politics in Wilmington and New Hanover County, N.C.—the Genesis of a Race Riot." Ph.D. dissertation, Kent State University, 1979.

———. "The Wilmington Riots of November 10, 1898," Master's thesis, Wake Forest University, 1963.

Ping, Nancy Reagan. "Music in Antebellum Wilmington and the Lower Cape Fear of North Carolina," Ph.D. dissertation, University of Colorado at Boulder, 1979.

The following list of secondary sources is by no means a comprehensive listing of the Lower Cape Fear's history, but it will provide a good start.

Barrett, John G. *Sherman's March through the Carolinas.* Chapel Hill: University of North Carolina Press, 1956.

Battle, Kemp P., "Letters and Documents Relating to the Early History of the Cape Fear." James Sprunt Historical Monograph, No. 4 (1903).

Burkhead, L.S. "History of the Difficulties of the Front Street Methodist Church, Wilmington, N.C. for the Year 1865." Trinity College Historical Society, *Papers,* VIII (1908-1909), 35-118.

Cashman, Diane; Poole, Jean; and New Hanover Medical Auxiliary Committee. *The Lonely Road: A History of the Physicks and Physicians of the Lower Cape Fear 1735-1976.* Wilmington, 1977.

Clifton, James M. "Golden Grains of White: Rice Planting on the Lower Cape Fear." *North Carolina Historical Review,* Vol. L, No. 4 (Oct. 1973), 365-391.

Cochran, Hamilton. *Blockade Runners of the Confederacy.* New York: Bobbs-Merrill Co., 1958.

Connor, R.D.W. "The Voyage of Verrazzano: The First Exploration of the N.C. Coast by Europeans." *North Carolina Booklet,* XVI (April 1917), 209-218.

Crittenden, Charles C. *The Commerce of North Carolina 1763-1789.* New Haven: Yale University Press, 1937.

Crow, Jeffrey J. *The Black Experience in Revolutionary N.C.* Raleigh: Division of Archives and History, 1977.

Cruickshank, Helen G., Ed. *John and William Bartram's America.* New York: The Devin-Adair Co., 1957.

Cutten, George B. (revised by Mary Reynolds Peacock). *Silversmiths of North Carolina.* Raleigh: Division of Archives and History, 1973.

deRosset, William Lord. *Pictorial and Historical New Hanover County and Wilmington, N.C. 1723-1938.* Wilmington, 1938.

Evans, W. McKee. *Ballots and Fence Rails: Reconstruction on the Lower Cape Fear.* Chapel Hill: The University of North Carolina Press, 1966.

Hall, Lewis Phillip. *Land of the Golden River.* Wilmington: Wilmington Printing Co., 1980.

Hall, Louise. "New Englanders at Sea: Cape Fear before the Royal Charter of 24 March 1662/63." *The New England Historical and Genealogical Register,* Vol. CXXIV (April 1970), 88-108.

Hewlett, Crockette W., and McEachern, Leora. *Attorneys of New Hanover County.* Wilmington, 1979.

Hewlett, Crockette W. *Between the Creeks: A History of Masonborough Sound 1735-1970.* Wilmington, 1971.

———. *Two Centuries of Art in New Hanover County.* Durham: Moore Publishing Co., 1976.

Howell, Andrew J. *The Book of Wilmington.* Wilmington: Wilmington Printing Co., 1930.

Johnson, F. Roy. *The Peanut Story.* Murfreesboro, N.C.: Johnson Publishing Co., 1964.

Johnson, Guion G. *Ante-Bellum North Carolina: A Social History.* Chapel Hill: University of North Carolina Press, 1937.

Kellam, Ida Brooks, and others. *Historic Wilmington-New Hanover County, N.C.* Wilmington, 1960.

Lee, E. Lawrence, Jr. "Days of Defiance: Resistance to the Stamp Act in the Lower Cape Fear." *North Carolina Historical Review,* XLIII, No. 2 (April 1966), 186-202.

———. *Indian Wars in North Carolina, 1663-1763.* Raleigh: Division of Archives and History, 1963.

———. *The Lower Cape Fear in Colonial Days.* Chapel Hill: The University of North Carolina Press, 1965.

———. "Old Brunswick: The Story of a Colonial Town." *North Carolina Historical Review,* XXIX, No. 2 (April 1952), 230-245.

Lee, Robert. *Blackbeard.* Winston-Salem: John F. Blair Pub., 1974.

Lefler, Hugh T., and Powell, William S. *Colonial North Carolina.* New York: Charles Scribner and Sons, 1973.

Lemmon, Sarah McCulloh. *Frustrated Patriots: North Carolina and the War of 1812.* Chapel Hill: University of North Carolina Press, 1973.

Lennon, Donald R. and Kellam, Ida Brooks, Eds. *The Wilmington Town Book 1743-1778.* Raleigh: Division of Archives and History, 1973.

MacMillan, Emma Woodward. *Wilmington's Vanished Homes and Buildings.* Raleigh, 1966.

Maffitt, Emma Martin. *The Life and Service of John Newland Maffitt.* New York: Bobbs-Merrill, 1906.

McEachern, Leora H., and Williams, Isabel M.

Wilmington-New Hanover Safety Committee Minutes 1774-1776. Wilmington, 1974.

McKoy, Elizabeth. *Early New Hanover County Records.* Wilmington, 1973.

_____ . *Early Wilmington Block by Block.* Wilmington, 1967.

McKoy, Henry Bacon. *Wilmington, N.C.--Do You Remember When?,* Greenville, S.C., 1957.

Merrens, Harry R. *Colonial North Carolina in the Eighteenth Century: A Study in Historical Geography.* Chapel Hill: University of North Carolina Press, 1964.

Moore, Louis T. *Stories Old and New of the Cape Fear Region.* Wilmington, L.T. Moore Memorial Fund, 1968.

Powell, William S. "Captain Blakeley's Daughter." *State,* Vol. IX, No. 5, July 5, 1941.

_____ . *The Correspondence of William Tryon,* (Vol. I-1758-1767, Vol. II-1768-1818). Raleigh, Division of Archives and History, 1980.

_____ . *North Carolina.* New York: W.W. Norton Co., 1977.

Quattlebaum, Paul. *The Land Called Chicora: The Carolinas under Spanish Rule with French Intrusions, 1520-1670.* Gainsville: The University of Florida Press, 1956.

Rankin, Hugh F. "The Moore's Creek Bridge Campaign, 1776." *North Carolina Historical Review,* XXX, No. 1 (Jan. 1953), 23-60.

_____ . *The Pirates of Colonial North Carolina.* Raleigh: Division of Archives and History, 1960.

Rights, Douglas L. *The American Indian in North Carolina.* Durham: Duke University Press, 1947.

Ross, Ishbel. *Rebel Rose.* New York: Harper and Brothers, 1954.

Ruark, Bryant W. "Some Phases of Reconstruction in Wilmington and the County of New Hanover." *Trinity College Historical Society, Papers,* XI (1915), 79-112.

Scharf, Thomas J. *History of the Confederate States Navy.* New York: Crown Publishers, Inc., 1977.

Schaw, Janet. Edited by Evangeline Andrews. *A Lady of Quality.* New Haven: Yale University Press, 1939.

Shaffer, E.T.H. *Carolina Gardens.* Chapel Hill: University of North Carolina Press, 1939.

Sprunt, James. *Chronicles of the Cape Fear River 1660-1916.* Raleigh: Edwards and Broughton Printing Co., (originally published 1916) 1961.

_____ . *Derelicts.* Wilmington, 1920.

_____ . *Tales of the Cape Fear Blockade.* Wilmington, 1905.

_____ . *Tales and Traditions of the Lower Cape Fear 1661-1896.* Wilmington, 1896.

Sprunt, James Laurence. *The Story of Orton Plantation.* Wilmington, 1958.

Thomas, Cornelius, M.D. *James Forte.* Wilmington, 1959.

Waddell, Alfred Moore. *A Colonial Officer and His Times.* Raleigh, Edwards and Broughton, 1890.

_____ . *History of New Hanover County, 1725-1780.* Wilmington, 1909.

_____ . *Some Memories of My Life.* Raleigh: Edwards and Broughton, 1908.

Warren, James Robert. "Wilmington, N.C.: A History in Towns." *Antiques,* Dec. 1980.

Watson, Alan D. *Money and Monetary Problems in Early North Carolina.* Raleigh, Division of Archives and History, 1980.

_____ . *Society in Colonial North Carolina.* Raleigh, Division of Archives and History, 1975.

Watson, Alan D.; Lawson, Dennis R.; and Lennon, Donald R. *Harnett, Hooper, and Howe: Revolutionary Leaders of the Lower Cape Fear.* Wilmington: Louis T. Moore Memorial Fund, 1979.

Wetmore, Ruth Y. *First on the Land: The North Carolina Indians.* Winston-Salem: John F. Blair, Publisher, 1975.

Williams, Isabel M., and McEachern, Leora H. *Salt.* Wilmington, Louis T. Moore Memorial Fund, 1973.

For 25 years the Lower Cape Fear Historical Society, Inc. has published its *Bulletin* three times a year. This publication has carried many worthwhile monographs on local history. Bound copies are available at the New Hanover County Library, the Randall Library at the University of North Carolina at Wilmington, and back issues are also available through the Society. The following articles were of particular value in researching *Cape Fear Adventure.*

Bacon, Ann Moore. "William and Margaret Moore Hill of Colonial Brunswick Town." Vol. XXIV, No. 3, May 1981.

Boney, Charles H. "The Historic District of Wilmington-Problems and Prospects." Vol. IX, No. 3, May 1966.

Bonner, Michael D. "The *Louisiana* and the Fort Fisher Fiasco of 1864." Vol. XV, No. 1, Sept. 1971.

Broadfoot, Mary Bason. "Kenan House." Vol. XV, No. 2, Jan. 1972.

_____ . "A Man with Two Countries: A Loyalist in Colonial Cape Fear." Vol. VIII, No. 3, May 1965.

_____ . "Thalian Hall." Vol. XIII, No. 2, Feb. 1970.

Broadfoot, Winston. "Perspective on the Blockade." Vol. IV, No. 1, Nov. 1960.

Crow, Jeffrey J. "Daniel Lindsay Russell and the Tradition of Dissent in the South." Vol. XX, No. 3, May 1977.

Debnam, John H. "Old Town Plantation Archaeological Project." Vol. XII, No. 3, May 1969.

DeMott, Mortimer. "Sojourn in Wilmington and the Lower Cape Fear, 1837." Vol. XXII, No. 3, May 1979.

Dolan, Diane. "A Yankee View of the Fall of Wilmington." Vol. XX, No. 2, Feb. 1977.

Flowers, John Baxton III. "Did Polly Slocumb Ride to the Battle of Moore's Creek Bridge?" Vol. XIX, No. 2, Feb. 1976.

Gurganious, Alfred and Susan Jane (Debose). "Letters-1861-1862." Vol. XVI, No. 3, May 1973.

Hall, Margaret T. "The Burgwin-Wright House." Vol. XXII, No. 2, Feb. 1979.

Hewlett, Crockette W. "New Hanover County Courthouse." Vol. XXI, No. 1, Oct. 1977.

Kellam, Ida Brooks. "The Tanyard House." Vol. X, No. 1, Oct. 1966.

MacMillan, Henry Jay. "Cape Fear Music of the 1850's." Vol. IV, No. 2, Feb. 1961.

_____ . "Cape Fear River Boats." Vol. VI, No. 2, Feb. 1963.

_____ . "Colonial Plantations of the Lower Cape Fear." Vol. XII, No. 2, Feb. 1969.

_____ . "The Goose Creek Men." Vol. III, No. 2, Feb. 1960.

Marcroft, Bobbie. "The Early Germans." Vol. XVIII, No. 2, Feb. 1975.

McEachern, Leora. "Accounts of the Moore's Creek Battle—1817 and 1822." Vol. XXV, No. 1, Oct. 1981.

McEachern, Leora H. and Walker, Ruth. "Pensioners Remember the War." Vol. XXIV, No. 2, Jan. 1981.

McEachern, Leora H. and Williams, Isabel M. "Miss Buie, the Soldier's Friend." Vol. XVIII, No. 1, Oct. 1974.

_____ . "The Prevailing Epidemic-1862." Vol. XI, No. 1, Nov. 1967.

_____ . "River Excursions 1864." Vol. XXI, No. 3, May 1978.

Shinn, Gerald H. "The Early History of Castle Haynes Plantation." Vol. XIII, No. 3, May 1970.

Stumpf, Vernon O. "Governor Josiah Martin: The Road to Cape Fear." Vol. XIX, No. 1, Oct. 1975.

_____ . "The Radical Ladies of Wilmington and Their Tea Party." Vol. XVI, No. 2, Feb. 1973.

Watson, Alan D. "Benjamin Smith: The Early Years of a North Carolina Governor." Vol. XXV, No. 2, Feb. 1982.

_____ . "Benjamin Smith: The General and the Governor." Vol. XXV, No. 3, May 1982.

_____ . "John Rutherfurd: Loyalist." Vol. XXI, No. 2, Feb. 1978.

_____ . "The Town Fathers of Early Wilmington, 1743-1775." Vol. XXIV, No. 1, Oct. 1980.

_____ . "William Dry: Passive Patriot." Vol. XVII, No. 1, Oct. 1973.

Index

Partners in Progress